RICHARD MUIR

The Villages of England

RICHARD MUIR

The Villages of England

with 151 illustrations, 73 in color

THAMES AND HUDSON

For Joanna, who grew up when I wasn't looking

On the title page:
Birstwith in Nidderdale, Yorkshire. The Greenwood family of Swarcliffe Hall,
upper right, were the patrons who provided the broach towered village church
and the neo-Gothic vicarage below it.

© *1992 Thames and Hudson Ltd, London*

First published in the United States in 1992 by
Thames and Hudson Inc., 500 Fifth Avenue,
New York, New York 10110

Library of Congress Catalog Card Number 91-66265

Typeset by Litho Link Ltd, Welshpool, Powys, Wales.
Printed and bound in Spain by Artes Graficas Toledo, S.A.
D.L.TO: 8-1992

Contents

Introduction

'The English village': there can be very few more evocative phrases in our language than this. When confronted with these words scarcely anybody in the English-speaking world will not respond instantly with colourful mental images of huddled cottages in mellow tones and narrow lanes alive with rustic characters. As far as they go, these images are real enough, but they are only a tiny facet of village life. The whole story has much more substance, depth and bite. It is a story of people who were once the mainstream of the national society. They lived in communities governed by survival; they were hardened by toil, sensed nothing of the present-day perception of village life and knew sentimentality only as a remote backwater of the mind.

This book has an unusual origin. *The English Village* was my first non-academic book. It was published in 1980 and its popularity encouraged me to become a full-time writer. A decade after publication only a small stock still remained and it would have been conventional for the publisher and author to consider either a reprint or a revised edition. Instead, I suggested a most unusual course: that I should completely rewrite and re-illustrate the book. Thames and Hudson agreed to this novel suggestion.

In the event, my approach to the task was even more unusual. I resolved that on no occasion during the writing would I refer to the original text. (I broke this resolution only once, to check a minor statistic.) I firmly believe that this approach was correct. The original book seemed coherent and any tinkering, involving various insertions and deletions in the text, would have undermined both the flow and the shades of meaning in the narrative.

Weobley, Hereford and Worcester, is the perfect 'Olde Worlde' English village of popular imagination, but most of the shops and hostelries are now divorced from their original function and directed at the tourist trade.

The English Village represented a step away from the conventional wisdom surrounding the subject. We had all been brought up to believe that in England villages were established by newly arrived hordes of Anglo-Saxon settlers and that such truly venerable villages were the norm throughout the countryside. When writing in 1978–79, I was beginning to find this interpretation of the evidence to be wearing rather thin. During the last decade much more information has emerged, particularly from the excavation of deserted medieval village sites, and the old explanation seems much thinner still. As a result, this book represents a further step away from the traditional – but still widely held – ideas. I have always been keen to pick the best brains and many of the most exciting ideas here have been gleaned from two old friends, Christopher Taylor and Tom Williamson. Chris helped me to develop a particular perspective on rural settlement, one which easily assimilates new evidence and ideas as they materialize.

Setting aside the archaeological issues, I find that more and more I am emphasizing the village as a community of people rather than as a collection of buildings. This is not so much an academic evolution as a personal reaction to the death of my native village, to which I returned after an absence of more than twenty years. Since it is more populous than it was before, 'death' might seem a highly inappropriate word. But in perhaps the most important sense, there is scarcely a village left which is not dead or dying. To my way of thinking, the essence of being a village was the intimate daily association between the people of the cottages and farmsteads and the land which surrounded them. Land and the way of living that it sustained created a culture, a dialect, an outlook, a meaning and an identity. These are the things that this book is about.

Less than a couple of centuries ago most of us were villagers. A book such as this would have been unnecessary because everybody knew what village life was all about. Now we are nearly all strangers to village life – and this is why it has been possible for a mythological counter-culture to emerge and take root. The strange thing is that as reality dies, so the myth is becoming reality. With sufficient affluence and inclination one can buy one's way into a village and mould it until it actually accords with the myth.

The old reality, the true one, is less accessible. My own village is less exposed to change than those to the south of the Trent. Even so the dialect of the dale, spoken everywhere in the 1950s, is scarcely ever heard, though well-manicured voices abound. Few people living here now have any notion of what village life was really like. Poverty was taken for granted, but did not seem to matter too much.

Contrary to current belief, gossip was not a major factor in communal life – if someone behaved badly one simply tended to avoid them. It was a narrow world, a somewhat male chauvinistic world, but one far richer than the one that survives.

By the early decades of the next century most members of my generation will be dead. And then there will be nobody left to recall what village life – I mean true village life – was really like. Members of the next generation will know only the myth. But at least they will know much more about the destiny of the English village than we do.

I cannot tell you much about its destiny, but this is what I know of its past. This is what made the English village what it was.

I Below the roots

When thinking of England from far-off places, from battlefields and from sickbeds, what visions of the homeland have people glimpsed? Prominent, often foremost, amongst the images of England has been, is and will be that of the village. It nestles gently in the patchwork quilt of its fields; its streets are mere lanes which wind between the walls of mellow stone or frames of blackened oak, and old-fashioned roses with shell-pink blooms surge over the lavender and thyme.

Is there any reality in these images? There is no doubt that the men and youths who left the leaf-hung lanes in carts and waggons bound for a county regiment and then the terrors of Ypres and the Somme knew villages which were not unlike those of our visions – and were ready to fight, perhaps to die, for a form of village England. But the coin had another side, for the army guaranteed regular meals, reliable employment and a chance to see the world beyond the market town – and anyone who could stomach the humiliations and exploitation of life on a typical farm or estate would find army discipline easy to accept. These men had memories of home but they did not live, as we do, in an age dominated and bewitched by images. (When the pub in the next village to my own was selected for use in a beer commercial it underwent a costly transformation from the unspoilt village pub that it was to an ad man's perception of what such a pub should really look like.) Almost every branch of the media is engaged in promoting an ever more idealized and idyllic image of the village. In the process, and contrary to intentions, the vision which the more discerning people receive is of an artificial and spineless place which, if it smells at all, has the sweet and cloying lavender odour found in

At Avebury, in Wiltshire, superstitious medieval villagers would not build within the sacred circle of stones and in fact destroyed many of them. But during the building of the late-Neolithic temple, villages for construction workers must have been built here.

National Trust shops and those village craft outlets which are packed with the cottage products of China and South Korea.

But here is a thought. Might it be that the village – the real village – was much more interesting than any of this? Could it be that instead of being a timeless and uncomplicated place the village was actually a fragile and complex kind of settlement, one which responded to every change in the circumstances of its times? And is it not likely that it was populated not by cardboard characters wishing to play the parts of yokel, milkmaid and worthy but by people of sensitivity, skill and passion? The answer to all these questions is 'Yes'.

This book can only be written according to the premise that the English village is an infinitely more interesting subject than the tedious old place that homesickness, whimsy and the media have created. The current vision of the village is not founded upon history but is rooted in the insecurity of a rootless society which has lost its links with the land. Like stray lambs in search of a ewe, people who have lost their sense of identity seek comfort and stability in the haven of the village of their dreams. But it is a mirage and in this book we are seeking the reality beyond the mirage.

Before farming was introduced about 7000 years ago, people lived by hunting, fishing, gathering wild roots, shoots and fruits and, perhaps, by herding reindeer. Such activities demanded much travel and much separation of families and communities, for a given area could support far fewer hunters than farmers so that any settlements would have been small and seasonal. But in hunting societies there is often a time of year when dispersed groups come together to socialize, exchange information, strengthen the tribal bonds and find husbands or wives. At such times temporary encampments form which are villages, if only in the loosest sense.

It is to the Middle Stone Age that we must look for evidence of the oldest village-like settlements in England. This era was heralded by a warming of the climate, which surpassed our modern levels of warmth. Broad-leafed forests expanded to displace the hardy, pioneering conifers, so that the entire strategy of human survival had to be remodelled to accord with the transformation of the environment.

Clan territories were established within which groups, often extended families, followed deliberate circuits. In the spring many moved up the wooded slopes, spending summer hunting on the open moors and fells. In autumn they descended through the woodland, where nuts were gathered in great quantities as winter provisions. The lean days of winter were passed at lakeshore and coastal settlements, where fishing could compensate for the shortages of hunting and scavenging, and it was at such places that gatherings and ceremonies were held.

For settlements that were more than hunting bases or meeting places to be formed, a new way of life had to develop, one which strengthened the bond between a community and the locality which supported it. This strengthening was made possible with the introduction to Britain of farming. The uncertainties in the evidence available still allow archaeologists to argue over whether Britain – by this time an island – experienced a wholesale invasion by European farmers or whether the foreign settlers were few in number and the idea of farming, along with seed grains and domesticated animals, reached the hunting and fishing communities of this offshore outpost through travel and trade and was adopted by them. Current thinking favours the latter viewpoint, but in any event the adoption of farming signalled a wholesale assault on the English wildwood. The first wave of clearances may have opened up areas with richer soils, perhaps signified by stands of lime, the queen of the wildwood. At first in this pioneering phase the settlements may have been impermanent, the felled timber being burned, crops sown in the ash-enriched soil and the clearings farmed briefly until the exhaustion of the soils signalled the abandonment of the farmsteads and a shift to new clearings. At the same time, hunting for game, large and small, remained important, so that between the sowing of crops and their harvest hunters may have left the homesteads, entrusting the tasks of weeding and scaring the forest animals from the rising wheat and barley to their spouses and children.

Numerous settlements of the period have been discovered, but generally the decay and destruction wrought by successive millennia of erosion, deposition and human activity have left little intact.

The settlement excavated on the summit of Carn Brea, near Redruth, provides some of the best insights into rural life in the New Stone Age. The first village was undefended, but around 3700 BC the rugged granite outcrops around the hilltop were linked by a great wall of boulders to defend an enclosure more than 8000 square yards (7000 square metres) in area. Here the ground was smoothed to form eleven platforms for dwellings. Some of these were built as lean-to structures against the stone rampart, with their remaining walls being of wattle woven between upright posts. They were around 8 feet (2.5 metres) wide and almost three times as long; storage pits sunk into the floors contained bag-shaped pots, while scooped-out hollows were used as working areas. The dwellings contained hearths but some cooking and socializing was done around campfires lit outside the rampart walls. The open-air hearths overlooked the farm plots from which stones had been gathered into cairns and where wheat was sown.

Amongst the stipple of farmsteads and hamlets in the English countryside of five and six thousand years ago there must also have been less prestigious villages. In Britain there is one such place which survives almost intact. It lies on the coast of the main island of the Orkneys at Skara Brae. The tight cluster of dwellings, walled in flagstone and linked by narrow alleyways, was home to a community who fished, gathered shellfish and farmed. Shortly after the seemingly sudden desertion of the village it was engulfed by sand dunes which eventually blew clear of the site in the nineteenth century to expose the homes that had survived with their stone flag furniture, hearths and bait tanks intact. However, life on the remote Orcadian coastline where farming conditions were difficult and driftwood provided the only source of timber must have been very different from that in the fertile farmland and woodland of the English plains and vales. So Skara Brae, beautifully preserved as it is, may not offer the best insights into the ancestral English village.

During the Bronze Age, which began around 2500 BC and lasted to about 650 BC, the English countryside was almost completely colonized and pacified, so that from most vantage points one would have seen a vast patchwork of hedged and ditched or walled fields interrupted by islands of woodland and marsh. The pattern of settlement seems to have developed along traditional lines, with the emphasis on farmsteads and hamlets but with small strongholds – 'mini-hillforts' – and palisaded palaces, and both open and defended villages, being interspersed in the pattern. Numerous excavated Bronze Age villages provide a clearer picture of rural life, but the most remarkable example known is far from being typical. Excavations are continuing at Flag Fen near Peterborough, where archaeological interest was aroused in 1982 when a lattice of timbers was seen below the surface of a Roman road which had been cut by a drainage ditch.

Soon the bases of upright posts which had supported huge timber long-houses were recognized. The buildings were about 20 feet (6 metres) wide and much longer (the full length remains to be exposed), while within the timber walls aisle posts in two rows helped to support the roof timbers and outside other rows of far shorter posts held up the eaves. The floors were of planks and carpentry debris dusted over with sand and fine gravel, while the long interiors seem to have been divided into stalls. Excavations may continue here but an imaginative reconstruction shows ten long-houses standing on the artificial island in the Fens.

Dartmoor preserves a number of Bronze Age village sites. This view of Grimspound looks from the ruined roundhouse to the gateway in the compound wall.

Since the excavations have not yet revealed the full dimensions of the long-houses, one cannot estimate the population of the village – though it was plainly a place of some importance. Far more typical of the period are small groupings of round houses set in paddocks and looking much, one supposes, like some East African hutted settlements of today. Seldom did these settlements grow to village proportions and most were the farmsteads of extended families or hamlets occupied by perhaps a score of relatives and close neighbours. The remains of such places tend to be accessible only to archaeologists, but in some little-disturbed upland places the landscape of Bronze Age life survives unburied and almost intact.

On Dartmoor the observant rambler can still discern the banks or 'reaves' which compartmentalized what was then a productive and well-populated countryside into territories and fields. The rings of stone which were once the low walls of dwellings are also visible. These can be found singly, in hamlet-sized clusters and, less often, in village groupings, some open and some enclosed – though not exactly fortified – by a stone compound wall. At Ryders Rings, South Brent, there was a substantial village perched at a height of 1200 feet (360 metres) in what is now bleak moorland. An elongated compound was built to enclose an area of about 6 acres (2.4 hectares) within a thick wall of granite boulders and rubble which may then have stood shoulder-high. Inside the wall a total of thirty-six circular dwellings was built, some of them free-standing and others abutting the compound, while a number of squarish yards or paddocks were also attached to the wall. Even if the dwellings were not all occupied at the same time the village at Ryders Rings must have been home to

Kestor is another Dartmoor village, this time of the Iron Age. Houses and pounds for animals were scattered amid a network of rectangular fields.

at least a hundred people: peasant farmers, like the other settlers on the moor.

A typical Iron Age village differed little from a Bronze Age one. Dwellings were still built on low, circular walls which were made of rubble in the uplands and of posts and wattle in the lowlands. They were crowned by tall, conical roofs of thatch and stood amongst their paddocks in unorganized clusters, while the living sites were pockmarked by the cylindrical pits in which grain was stored. (The old archaeologists mistook these pits for homes and believed that Iron Age folk lived in holes in the ground!) The pattern of settlement, however, had become more diverse. The change reflected not only the increasingly stratified nature of society but also the level of tension between communities infested with aristocratic warriors who were competing for resources in lands which farming had pressed to the limits of efficiency and expansion. While some settlements stood exposed and undefended, others were ringed by banks, ditches and thorn hedges. Meanwhile, on the summits and scarp crests and even on less favourable terrain, formidable defence-works had appeared, the hillforts, many of which contained substantial village-sized populations.

One Iron Age village was discovered when part of the new Stansted airport was being built. It belonged to a late stage in the period, with settlement beginning around 75 BC. Two circular dwellings were erected along with a rectangular granary which was

Left: a reconstruction of the village of Stansted, Essex, showing its late development (c. 50 AD) with seven dwellings, a granary raised on legs and a shrine in the centre.

Bratton and Edington, in Wiltshire; the villages are dominated by the ramparts of the great hillfort of Bratton Castle.

carried above the reach of damp and vermin on six supporting posts. In the middle of the century the little settlement was fortified. Seven dwellings and a granary were built with post and wattle walls which were encircled by drainage ditches to catch the rainwater dripping from the thatch. At the centre of the compound was a shrine.

In the centuries before the foundation of the settlement at Stansted, villages of a different kind had been developing inside great girdles of ramparts and ditches on many an English hilltop. It would be wrong to regard the hillforts of the Iron Age simply as fortified villages. The enormous investment of time and manpower needed to create the defenceworks was far greater than any ordinary village could muster or merit. The hillforts were citadels which dominated and protected the surrounding territory and its farming communities, but their role in Iron Age life was more complicated than this. Some contained numerous granaries, to which farm produce was despatched as a form of tribute to the chieftain, who then redistributed the produce as a kind of largesse.

The hillfort villages varied considerably in size and in layout. At Croft Ambrey, in the Welsh Marches, an imposing hillfort was built to fortify the crest of an escarpment around 650 BC. The interior was packed with rectangular buildings which were supported on corner posts and set out, row after row, in neat streets. This unusual arrangement has caused much controversy, for the buildings have variously been interpreted as granaries, as dwellings, and even as barracks. Some at least were granaries since the building style seems identical to granaries positively identified at other sites. The organization of hillfort interiors into streets lined by rectangular buildings has also been discovered at Credenhill Camp, another hillfort of the Welsh Marches, and at Danebury in Hampshire. More commonly, the dwellings were round houses which were scattered in a haphazard fashion within the defences, as at Maiden Castle in Dorset. At Hod Hill, also in Dorset, the hillfort was packed with round houses and must have supported a population of at least 1000 people.

At the great majority of hillforts no obvious evidence of dwellings can be found though such evidence frequently emerges during excavations. At Hambledon Hill in Dorset around 175 Iron Age houses have been recognized and at Midsummer Hill in the Welsh Marches there were approximately 200. Other hillfort villages were generally much smaller, like the twenty dwellings at Beacon Hill in Hampshire or the ten at Abbotsbury in Dorset.

Given the predominance of the smaller settlements, the existence of a village in the Bronze and Iron Ages was a slightly unusual

This scene at Houghton, near Huntingdon, epitomizes the gentle myth of Village England.

occurrence. Most village dwellings, however, were similar to those built as farmsteads and hamlets and, as in the centuries to follow, many villages grew from humble beginnings. The little village at Thorpe Thewles near Stockton-on-Tees developed from the nucleus of a stockaded farmstead that was built around 200 BC.

Most homes were circular and had no distinct room divisions. A hearth burned in the centre of the earthen floor and family members must have reclined with their backs to the low, curving wall and their feet towards the fire as they gazed towards each other across the glowing peat and talked of work, gossiped about neighbours or listened to a storyteller. Though strange to modern eyes, the houses were often quite well-built, consisting mainly of a great smoke-wreathed cone of thatch supported on a forest of converging rafters. Such houses were frequently much more substantial and durable than the shanties occupied by medieval village peasants. The farmstead at Thorpe Thewles stood for a century before it was dismantled to make way for the round houses of the village.

The villagers of the Iron Age were not pioneers but lived in a farmed countryside which was already old and which displayed the traces of many phases of human endeavour. They were not free and must have rendered tribute in kind or in labour to their warrior chieftains. Perhaps the greatest barrier to our understanding of life in the prehistoric village derives from our habit of regarding prehistoric people as bizarre savages dwarfed by the wilderness in which they lived. Yet the Iron Age and Bronze Age countrysides were largely carefully managed farmlands and their inhabitants were people biologically indistinguishable from ourselves. If we could transplant a group of Victorian farmworkers into an Iron Age village they would find the transition relatively easy and could instantly contribute to the work of the community, soon recognizing the antiquity of many of the facets of farming lore and practices which they had inherited.

The prehistoric village was several broad strides removed from the village of our visions and memories. There were no high streets or back lanes, no greens and seldom any sign of a coherent layout. The neatly planned hillfort villages, like Croft Ambrey, were very much the exceptions and in other places only the constraints imposed by the encircling palisade or ditch affected the distribution of dwellings, paddocks and pits.

We should not seek the ancestry of the historical English village in the villages of prehistory — not least because the ancient villages were relatively ephemeral places. Some existed for only a single generation, some for a century or so, though few endured for more than three or four centuries, even though the recolonization of long-abandoned sites often took place. As yet we do not know why villages and hamlets which appear to have been perfectly serviceable should have been deserted as a matter of habit. This practice is still common in several of the so-called primitive societies that survive today and it is usually caused by concern about the build-up of infection and parasites at long-settled sites. But if this were the case in Iron Age England then why did medieval villages, generally badly built and insanitary places, tend to be occupied permanently unless they fell as victims to particular assaults? Needless to say, the 'removal habit' was not without its costs. The ancient dwellings consumed enormous quantities of valuable coppice and woodland timber and masses of wheatstraw thatch and could be surrounded by ditches, banks and palisades; village-making involved much toil and many resources. And yet the abandonment of villages was the norm throughout the prehistoric period, even though we have still to interpret the logic behind the desertions.

Farming had intensified the bond between people and place but village and society were different in ancient times. Prehistoric settlements were less deeply rooted; they could endure for generations but seldom for many centuries. Family and tribe attracted greater loyalty than any sense of a village-based community – while some hamlets and small villages must have been inhabited entirely by the members of a single extended family. People lived in villages when it seemed convenient to do so, but they seem to have quit the old home with few qualms when it suited them.

The prehistoric era ended with the Roman invasion in 43 A D. Seven or eight centuries would pass before the foundations of village England would be laid, while the Dark Ages, Middle Ages and later centuries would come and go before anyone imagined that the village was anything more than a place for poor landworkers to sleep in.

Overleaf:
One of the Bronze Age dwellings at Grimspound, Dartmoor; ruined houses and field walls at the once populous Bronze Age village of peasants and tin-miners on the slopes of Rough Tor, Dartmoor; and an Iron Age farmstead painstakingly reconstructed at Butser Hill, near Petersfield.

2 Villages of the Roman rise and fall

We now enter the periods of the Roman empire and of the Saxon settlement of England which followed. Traditionally, these times are credited with the birth of village England. In fact the evidence of archaeology does not seem to support such a notion – even though enormous changes were taking place in the countryside. In the course of the Roman occupation villages, formerly rather uncommon, became numerous and they developed in a remarkably diverse range of shapes and sizes. However, in the years of chaos and calamity which resulted from the British leaders' failure to replicate the stable government of imperial times, most of the Roman villages must have been deserted. And so the foundations of village England had to be laid anew.

The Roman armies conquered a land which was rich in grain and livestock but which had reached the limits of its potential under the turbulent regime of the rival tribal kings. The imperial administrators imposed the rule of law and a centralized government – and in the climate of peace and commerce which resulted a variety of rural settlements multiplied. Farming technology was advanced with the importation of ploughs of a superior design. Meanwhile, the demand for farm produce at the military bases, in the continental empire and in the new towns developing in the British colony assured a market for all that the native farmers could produce. The new settlements which erupted throughout the countryside were not occupied by Romans or even planned by them, but they represented a native British response to the changes which their conquerors had enforced. Real Romans, mainly part of an élite of commanders and administrators, were few in Britain. The great fortresses and far-flung

Chysauster, in Cornwall, existed before the Roman occupation but continued to be occupied during that time. Here we are looking at the central courtyard of one house, with inward-facing chambers opening off it.

outposts of the army of occupation were manned by soldiers drawn from three continents and all parts of the vast empire, some of whom were settled in urban communities of veterans as their service lives expired, while the mansions or villas which were the headquarters of farming estates were frequently owned by Romanized native aristocrats.

England was effectively divided into upland and lowland zones, the division between them being very roughly marked by the Fosse Way from Dorchester to Lincoln. In the upland zone the territories were policed and pacified and resources of minerals and livestock were exploited, although most features of indigenous life continued much as before. The process of Romanization went much further in the civilized lowlands, where towns flourished, villas appeared and where most people were closely involved with the economy of the empire. Everywhere, however, the new rural settlements were mushrooming. In parts of the East Midlands or along the rich margins of the Fens a rambler who chose to walk from one settlement to the next might pass through half a dozen different farmsteads, hamlets or villages in the course of just an hour of walking. In a few well-favoured localities the number would rise to eight or ten. Even in the bleak hills of Northumberland farming hamlets could be found at distances of just a mile and a half apart.

Had the Romans been masterminding this vigorous new colonization of the countryside, we can be sure that the settlements produced would have had planned and rather stereotyped layouts, like the Roman towns and camps. In fact, we encounter a remarkable diversity of shapes and sizes and it is clear that the administrators allowed economic and social forces to shape the patterns. Their concerns were with peace, produce and the payment of taxes. There was no typical Roman village.

Many villages were sited along or beside ditched trackways and their dwellings were associated with little enclosures, paddocks or garden plots. One at Chisenbury Warren, near Enford in Wiltshire, is an example. A trackway formed the village street, which was almost half a mile in length. Along it around eighty dwellings were situated, while forks at either end of the trackway may have bordered common pastures or greens. Some villages echoed the indigenous tradition of unorganized growth, but in other cases it is clear that the Roman enthusiasm for orderly planning had influenced native thinking. A good example was recently excavated at Claydon Pike in Gloucestershire. The site was settled in the Iron Age, but soon after the Roman conquest a new village was set out upon a straight and partly metalled road which then formed its main street.

Overleaf:
Horningsea, on the edge of the Cambridgeshire fens, has a complicated history. The locality supported a mass-producing pottery industry in Roman times, while later a village formed around the nucleus of a minster church.

The buildings were arranged in six rectangular blocks which were divided by side streets, while in the centre of the settlement there was an open area, comparable to a market square and measuring 152 by 90 feet (46 × 27 metres). The sides of the square were lined by domestic buildings, some of which seem to have been farmsteads. Places such as this were without precedent in prehistoric Britain, but planned villages and villages with greens do not seem to have been unusual in Roman England.

There were also industrial villages, like the pottery-making centres of Cambridgeshire, with buildings blackened by the smoke from the kilns, and other places – roadside market and service centres and tribal capitals – which hovered in the marchlands between village and town.

In yet other places, shielded by distance and terrain from the main forces of change, older habits still held sway. One of them, now beautifully preserved, was Chysauster in Cornwall. This village of 'courtyard houses' receives thousands of visitors each year. It was founded around 100 BC and continued to be occupied during the Roman period. The dwellings were of a peculiar indigenous Cornish type, each being roughly oval in plan and consisting of a number of stone-walled chambers arranged around an open central courtyard. Eight dwellings were arranged in pairs, the members of each pair being separated by the track which formed the village street, while a ninth house lay down a short alleyway; walled garden plots were attached to the houses. The excavation of the site revealed stone querns, which were used for grinding grain, but the Roman inhabitants of Chysauster may have combined tin working with their farming operations. Just to the south of the village was a contemporary example of a Cornish 'fogou', a stone-lined tunnel which may have been used for storage and for rituals of some kind. Though the people of Chysauster may have traded tin with the Roman empire, their village was built in a traditional style. Other villages which preserved the native concepts of home life flourished at countless places in the uplands of England and Wales, with the seemingly disorganized clusters of roundhouses and paddocks occurring at site after site throughout upland Britain from Cumbria down to Cornwall.

Two models competed for the attention of the village home-builders of Roman England. There was the homegrown model, a roundhouse with a central hearth, no windows, low walls and a tall, conical roof of thatch and there was the Roman ideal, a rectangular building with door, windows and a gabled roof that could be thatched or clad in clay tiles. Within particular localities there were

Carn Euny, Cornwall: one of the large circular dwellings which had access to the underground passage or 'fogou' of the village.

devotees of both the old and new traditions. At the farmstead which nestled inside the earthworks still surviving at Woodcutts in Dorset, successive generations of farmers remained wedded to a way of life which had scarcely changed since Iron Age times until quite late in the Roman period, although eventually one adventurous occupant paid to have a tiled roof and walls of painted plaster. Meanwhile in Wessex, villages of rectangular Roman-style houses had appeared at places like Studland and Chisenbury Warren in Dorset and on Overton Down near Avebury.

In the case of Studland, a cluster of timber huts of the Iron Age type were built just a few years after the Roman landings. A generation later the Studland villagers were converted to the new building fashions and they replaced their old houses with new ones which still had timber walls but were built on stone footings to a rectangular design. These homes must have been found to be both satisfactory and serviceable, for they remained in use for three centuries. In some places, affluence and a thorough conversion to Roman values enabled village dwellings to boast such sophistications as door locks, windows and roof tiles, while in others the progress was more hesitant. At Odell in Bedfordshire, for example, traditional roundhouses were rebuilt on several occasions during the occupation and it was not until the third century that the site was commandeered by a rectangular stone building with five rooms.

The changes in architectural fashion had great repercussions on social life. In the old roundhouses there were no room divisions, although different segments of the circular floor space were set aside

*The remains of two
Romano-British villages
in Cornwall:
Chysauster (above) and
Carn Euny (right).*

for sleeping, working and domestic activities. The rectangular village houses were often two-roomed cottages, and at Studland one of these rooms would serve as domestic accommodation and the other as a byre for the family livestock. For peasants the cottage living-room was probably still the home base of an extended family, crowded as it may have been. Meanwhile, the family's ancestral overlord was, as likely as not, living in a nearby villa in considerable comfort. He had not just one room in which all the functions of life were enacted but ranges of different, special-purpose rooms. He may well have slackened the bonds of kinship binding the group together, for his eyes were now turned towards Rome and the luxury and progress it symbolized.

It is very likely that many flourishing English villages stand upon the sites of Roman villages and hamlets – the Roman settlements speckled the countryside so densely that it would be odd if it were otherwise. Even so, for a village to have lived *continuously* from the Roman period to the present, it would have had to endure through what was perhaps the most traumatic, calamitous and change-ridden period in our history. Any village which could have survived throughout the Dark Ages was a very tough customer indeed – and a very lucky one too. There is no doubt that many facets of the medieval countryside had their origins in Roman times and that the Roman legacy influenced later landscapes in a variety of subtle ways. Some English villages may well be descended from Roman villages, hamlets or villas but these are bound to be a minority.

Around 410 AD the Romans realized that they could no longer hope to secure Britain and the islanders were advised to protect themselves as best they could. The British leaders responded by quitting the failing empire.

The screen of history darkens and when it clears again we see England divided into several pagan Saxon kingdoms. Some of the ruling dynasties have Celtic rather than English names, but English has become the dominant language. The writers and teachers of the old history almost all agreed that it was during this misty period of Saxon colonization that life began for the majority of English villages. The saga of the Saxon founding fathers was repeated with great confidence, so that readers and listeners might have imagined that it was founded on rock-hard facts rather than upon speculation and supposition. When archaeology came to grips with the Dark Ages, it painted a completely different picture. It showed that the Roman countryside was not a wooded wilderness dotted (inexplicably) with villas. Instead it was an intensely agricultural landscape with few woods – and one which was worked so hard that in some places watercourses were choked with plough soil flushed by the winter rains from eroding fields. It also revealed that the time of the Saxon settlement which followed was not one of pioneering colonization but a period when old farmland was falling into disuse, when thorn trees encroached on the grazings and when new woods spread across the sites of once lively Roman settlements.

Some authorities now believe that while the British population numbered millions, the Saxon settlers amounted to no more than several thousand. The native British could never have been exterminated or evicted to the highlands of the north and west and the Saxon triumph was a linguistic one. After all, English now provides a lingua franca in countries like India and Kenya, where the British élite was always a tiny minority.

Far from having taken over the choicest sites, the newcomers, doubtless regarded as uncouth peasants and dangerous mercenaries by the Romanized majority, often settled in the less inviting places. Hired soldiers may have been billeted in derelict hillforts, while retired legionaries or reformed raiders settled the poorer land on the margins of estates. Sometimes the sites of crumbling villas were resettled, as at Latimer in Buckinghamshire or Barton Court in Oxfordshire; at both places humble timber buildings were erected amongst the ruins, occupied for more than a century and then abandoned.

In other places, however, the newcomers and the natives lived together. During the last stages of the Roman empire in Britain pagan Saxon mercenaries and their British wives lived on the outskirts of Cambridge, while recent excavations at Heslerton in the Vale of Pickering have shown that, early in the fifth century, the indigenous community at this long-established village was peacefully joined by Saxons who may have emigrated from southern Denmark. By 450 AD the old village had become waterlogged and all the villagers moved to a new site about half a mile away, where buildings quite similar to those discovered at Saxon settler sites were erected.

At West Stow in Suffolk a small pagan Saxon community was established in an area of poor, sandy soils. Rather than slaughtering their British neighbours and evicting them from their homes, the English settlers seem to have engaged in peaceful trade. The excavations accomplished at West Stow revealed buildings similar to those found at other early Saxon sites – buildings whose nature and function are still debated. There were six halls and sixty-eight 'sunken huts' built here between the fifth and eighth centuries.

The sunken huts were small rectangular buildings with their floors

scooped out to form hollows which could be just a few inches or almost three feet (one metre) below ground level. Such huts might be crude buildings without walls and covered in tent-like roofs of branches and thatch or they could be more homely, with boarded floors and roofs carried above walls of upright planks. The excavators at West Stow made a distinction between the sunken huts and the more imposing and conventional halls, which also had plank-built walls and gabled roofs of thatch.

At different Saxon village sites the ratios between well-built halls and sunken huts vary greatly. Mucking in Essex was one of the first sites to be settled by incoming Saxons. Here around 190 sunken huts have been counted but only ten other buildings. They were arranged into two neighbouring villages with two cemeteries where more than 800 burials and cremations were made between the fifth and early eighth centuries. It has been argued that from around 400 AD onwards Saxons arrived here as armed auxiliaries invited by the Roman authorities, perhaps to guard the Thames estuary, but as the century progressed the incomers came as peasant settlers.

Although the villages have been the subjects of a meticulous excavation between 1965 and 1981, the experts disagree about their function. Some see Mucking as a great transit camp which gave temporary accommodation to settlers bound for the interior, others as a more conventional collection of peasant homesteads, while to others still Mucking was the seasonal abode of shepherds.

By no means all the dwellings at West Stow or Mucking were in use at any single time, but even so the impression is of unplanned and sprawling villages. If only the six halls at West Stow were used as dwellings, then it was merely a small village, but if there were people living in the huts here and at Mucking, then large village populations would have been supported. At other English settlements, like Catholme in Staffordshire and Chalton in Hampshire, the ratios between the different types of buildings were completely different. Catholme had only six huts but fifty-eight houses and Chalton had but two huts and fifty houses.

The more that we explore the villages of Saxon England, the more complicated the subject seems to become. The village site at Catholme in Staffordshire was occupied from around 500 AD until the first half of the tenth century, though at no time did it resemble most conventional impressions of the English village. It seems to have consisted of about seven farms. Each farm was enclosed by a palisade containing a large dwelling house and outbuildings and workshops, sometimes including sunken huts and raised granaries. Here the sunken huts seem to have served as spinning and weaving

A reconstructed pagan Saxon building at West Stow, in Suffolk.

33

sheds, while the houses were built in three different styles, including a large boat-shaped building. Chalton in Hampshire was a hill-crest village which was occupied during the sixth and seventh centuries. Again there was an association between larger houses, which were certainly used as dwellings, and smaller buildings, which could have been workshops, stores or shelters for the less fortunate members of the community. The dwelling houses were rectangular, 25 to 45 feet (8 to 14 metres) in length and 15 to 22 feet (4½ to 6½ metres) in width.

At Cowdery's Down near Basingstoke a Roman site was resettled by a group of twenty colonists. Before the place was abandoned, around 800 AD, the population of the village had increased more than threefold. Much, but not all, of the development took place inside one or other of two compounds and a total of eighteen major buildings and two huts were erected, not all being in use at the same time. The houses were very solid rectangular buildings of upright posts and planks. And while the timber-walled constructions at Chalton seem to have been built with 'hipped' roofs (or inward-sloping gables), the roofs here may have either been hipped or else been carried on vertical gable walls, with the main doorways being placed in the gable wall rather than in the long walls as at Chalton. The substantial nature of the houses at Cowdery's Down led the excavators to speculate that this may not have been a humdrum peasant village but the base of the local ruling class. Heslerton was a little different again. It also had well-built timber-framed houses, some having two storeys and planked floors, their walls being formed of pairs of planks set upright in the ground. The dwellings were associated with sunken huts where items of spinning and weaving equipment were discovered.

The early Saxon villages showed very little sign of organization in their layouts and the use of compounds or palisades to surround groups of buildings echoes the archaic practices of Iron Age times. There were no orderly rows of cottages of the kind so common in medieval villages. Rather the villages seem to have consisted of loose clusters of farmsteads, each farmhouse being surrounded by the huts and sheds which served as workshops, accommodation for workers or slaves and outbuildings.

There is one factor common to the villages which have been described: all were abandoned after only a couple of centuries of occupation. Early in the tenth century Catholme was derelict and a new system of fields was set out across its site. Chalton was deserted in the seventh century and the villagers dispersed to several neighbouring hamlets. West Stow was abandoned to the drifting

sands of the Brecklands. The villages were not deserted after dramatic or violent events. Instead, the old prehistoric habits of colonization, a few centuries of occupation and then abandonment still seem to have held sway. Possibly a few existing English villages have been settled continuously since the fifth or sixth century. The traces of a Saxon sunken hut have been unearthed at the deserted medieval village of Wharram Percy in the Yorkshire Wolds, but this need not prove an early origin.

Much of Saxon England consisted of landscape such as this, near Luppitt, in Devon; hamlets and farmsteads set within a network of older fields.

On the whole, the centuries following the collapse of Roman power emerge not as a dynamic and formative age but as a time of decay when more settlements contracted or failed than were founded. Plagues, some perhaps of quite horrifying severity, swept across the countryside and few people could realistically aspire to more than the most basic levels of survival. By the time of King Alfred, England may have supported less than half the number of people living here at the end of the Roman occupation.

If we could enter the mind of an early Saxon villager we would probably discover outlooks and priorities which have as much in common with those of the prehistoric farmer as with those of the medieval peasant. The village has no church or temple but religious beliefs are still an important force. Beyond the village bounds there is a cemetery where the dead are variously buried or cremated. For the Saxon villager, it is important to be buried with grave goods for use in the afterlife – even if this means interring a valuable sword or set of spears beside the body of a warrior. Religion embraces a host of Germanic deities often perceived in a rather hazy manner – but people agree that ghosts are real and frightening and they perform all the rituals deemed necessary, such as the decapitation of corpses or bodies being weighted down with boulders, in order to prevent spirits from walking.

The world of the villagers is but a locality and this locality provides almost all the essentials of life. The cultural stage has shifted again. Just as the Celtic arena gave way to that of the Roman world, so the Roman theatre of action has been supplanted by a North Sea sphere of trade and influence. There are scarcely any towns left now. The crumbling ruins of the Roman centres and the old villa sites, where nettles encroach on mounds of rubble and mortar and the snout of the plough rattles fragments of roof tile, have become the subjects of myth and legend. This is not a time of hopeful endeavour but one pervaded by grim pessimism. People are aware that an age of greatness has passed away and feel that the end of the world is near. There is no sense of national identity and no feeling of belonging to anything other than a local community. Villagers have been told that some of their forbears migrated from a distant land beyond the sea, but whether the land they now inhabit is an island or not, they neither know nor really care. Most villagers are more British than Saxon but they speak an Anglo-Saxon dialect, the tongues of southern Denmark, the Frisian islands and the Low Countries having been simplified to facilitate conversations with the native people. But all around the village the hills and streams are still known by their Celtic names. Culture varies enormously from one locality to another and each village is a simmering melting pot in which the British and Germanic ingredients bubble together in different quantities, spiced with the age-old local qualities.

Contacts are far fewer than before, though occasionally news is brought by a salt trader, a wandering smith or a noble warrior returning from pillage and slaughter in a neighbouring kingdom.

As in earlier ages, society is dominated by those who can combine claims to have nobles and gods amongst their ancestors with a capacity for intrigue and violence. They drink, hunt and boast a good deal and lay claim to all the surplus farm production. This rent or tribute allows them to buy a few exotic trinkets, yet they live in conditions which we would regard as filthy and squalid. Village society is impoverished (by our standards) but rigidly stratified, with slaves occupying the lowest rung on the social ladder. Sometimes slaves have their own settlements, those giving rise to the numerous 'Carlton' place-names which survive today. The Saxon villager does not step out of his cottage on to the high street or green and his village lacks the compact intimacy of later villages. Rather, he goes from his farmstead to a compound or yard which contains sheds and workshops. Beyond the surrounding fence or hedge muddy tracks weave around the handful of neighbouring farmsteads. It is a place without form or landmarks. Villages are still a small minority amongst rural settlements. England remains a land of farmsteads and hamlets.

3 The birth of village England

Between the arrival in Kent of Augustine and his Christian mission, in 597, and the compilation of Domesday Book, almost five centuries later, the English countryside experienced a remarkable transformation. The Domesday rural landscape looked more like the one we know today than the one that had existed in Augustine's time. As the Christian missionaries moved between the different English kingdoms, they saw fieldscapes inherited from Iron Age and even earlier times. These were broken here and there by groups of rectangular Roman fields or by new clearings hacked into the thorns and woodland which had advanced as Roman life decayed. They saw plenty of farmsteads and hamlets, but in most places villages were small in size and few in number. When William the Conqueror's forces explored their new kingdom in 1066, they also found some countrysides that were ancient, but many others in which compact young villages sat at the centres of vast spreads of communal ploughland and in which most traces of the world of the Roman villa and farmstead had been erased. It is only recently that we have been able roughly to date the rural revolution caused by the adoption of communal farming in open fields, while the ways in which village, church and manor slotted into this jigsaw of change are still being explored.

Some archaeologists call it 'the Mid-Saxon shuffle' – a period around the eighth and ninth centuries when old hamlets, farmsteads and the incoherent little villages of the earlier Saxon years were abandoned and when their populations flooded into new villages of a different kind. The old settlements were impermanent – but thousands of the new ones still survive today.

Okeford Fitzpaine, in Dorset, has cottages of the seventeenth century and seems to epitomize the stability of the 'Olde Worlde' village. But these cottages are built over a former green which was itself preceded by the original village, which was clustered around the church.

Such huge transformations take place in the countryside at certain times in history. It is interesting to consider the conditions under which such revolutions can occur. They can happen when massive immigration and technological advance are combined with surging national vitality, as with the settlement of the American interior. And they can occur when countries are subordinated to the visions of a ruthless dictator, as with Stalin's collectivization drive or Ceaușescu's more recent assault upon Romanian rural traditions. But the England of the eighth century seems to have been the most unlikely setting for such a revolution. There was still no great hunger for land and the countryside supported less than half the number of people that it had sustained in Roman times. Neither was there a single omnipotent leader; rival dynasties were still competing when the first Viking raiders set foot upon English soil in 787 to launch a new era of terror and uncertainty.

Until quite recently our understanding of early village history rested upon two seemingly substantial pillars: the evidence of place-names and the information garnered from Domesday Book. To understand villages now we must cease to rely on these pillars and begin our work afresh. The evidence will not be discarded but it must be reappraised. A new and more accurate vision of the birth of village England is rooted in the clues produced by excavations at village sites. The interpretation of the clues involves topics which are still hazy and uncertain: the effects of open field farming, the organization of the manor and the influence of the church.

Modern archaeology has shown that around the time of King Alfred and the Danish settlement, or a little before, large numbers of impermanent hamlets, farmsteads and small villages were being abandoned and their populations were drifting into new villages. The surviving literature of late Saxon times shows that the vocabulary of open field farming, with its many terms to describe all kinds of land and land use, had become entrenched in the English language. All this seems to tell us that in some parts of England at least the old countrysides of small fields and scattered farmsteads had given way to new ones where compact villages sat amongst their communally worked fields. It is also tempting to suppose that the changes in the pattern of settlement were wrought by the innovation in the organization of farming.

The birth pangs of village England must have created great social and scenic changes. The events were revolutionary, but the revolution was not sudden or comprehensive. New villages continued to be created through the Norman and the Plantagenet periods. Frequently it emerges that there was no Saxon phase of occupation and villages were not settled until the twelfth or thirteenth centuries. By this time the population of England was creeping closer to the level that had been supported in Roman times and settlements were being created which either increased the population of long-established areas or re-established communities in less inviting settings, such as those that had been deserted for many centuries.

Open field farming was a complicated but effective form of agriculture which varied in its details from place to place. Where it came from, we do not know, but it certainly was not introduced by the Saxon settlers.

For the system to operate, a large expanse of land was needed, plus the authority to subdivide and reallocate the expanse. Land suitable for arable farming was partitioned into two, three or several more great fields, the fields into blocks or 'furlongs'; and the furlongs into ribbons, which were strips or 'selions'. Damp land in the valley bottoms supported hay meadow and the meadow was also divided into strips or 'doles', while the village herds of sheep and cattle grazed on the heath, open pasture or marches which constituted the common or 'waste'. The smooth running of the system depended on the entire farming community submitting itself to complicated rules and regulations. It involved not only major decisions about crop rotations and task-sharing but also tiny details, like rights of grazing on narrow ribbons of grass dividing some strips. It was operated by bondsmen of at least three distinct ranks, each rank having its own particular obligations, and was buttressed by an intricate body of regulations and fines.

With the adoption of an open field system the entire village community became locked into an elaborate calendar of mutual obligations. Farm production was increased, with land which had been ploughed intermittently being released for use as valuable permanent pasture, while extra grazing was also available upon whichever of the plough fields was being fallowed. Meanwhile peasants, who may previously have been free to make their own decisions about the farming of the lands which they tenanted, found themselves as small cogs in the wheels of village farming. Each small task that they performed had to be synchronized in the cycle of communal effort. Given the complexity of the undertakings, there must have been great advantages in having the landforce concentrated in a village dormitory at the heart of the little empire of farmland.

Much about the emergence of open field farming remains mysterious and the topic has probably been the subject of more expert study and controversy than any other in early English history.

The system was so elaborate and the fieldscapes that it created so different from those that had gone before that it is hard to regard it as the result of gradual evolution. During its adoption the political climate was turbulent. Despite the fact that no king was powerful enough to impose the adoption of open field farming upon his realm, the new system seems to have spread across England quite rapidly. Whatever its origins, it seems to have been adopted and imitated by the local lords on estate after estate.

So far there are just two significant clues about the origins of open field farming. Firstly, while the typical medieval field strip was around 220 yards (200 metres) in length, archaeologists working in several different parts of England have found the medieval strips underlain by older 'long strips' which could be half a mile or more in length. The implications of this are still to be unravelled. Secondly, historians studying the names of tenants recorded in medieval manorial documents have discovered that originally village land holdings were set out in such an intricate way that each peasant at work in his field strips had the same neighbours on either side as he did when at home in his hovel. Such an elaborate arrangement, which also existed in some Scandinavian lands, could only be the creation of planning of a most methodical and detailed kind.

Perhaps the local lords, who certainly had the power to uproot their tenants and resettle them in purpose-built agricultural villages, were the architects of the new system. As to the date of the changes, they certainly did not occur in the period of the Saxon settlement, when the old fields of Roman Britain remained in use, while the literature of the late Saxon period shows that the vocabulary of open field farming, with its specialized words for different facets of the fieldscape, had by then been adopted and become entrenched in the language of England.

At school most children learn a misleadingly simple version of open field farming. It is often called 'the three field system'; in fact there might only be two great fields – though as many as nine could exist. Also it is assumed that open field farming was ubiquitous in Saxon and medieval England. In reality, very extensive parts of the kingdom were never affected and the old pattern of small fields worked from scattered farmsteads and hamlets persisted and still persists to this day. This might not be surprising if the areas of ancient countryside were confined to the relatively barren uplands where patches of good plough soil were few and far between, but ancient countryside covers much of lowland England. Thus one can pass from parts of Cambridgeshire, with big villages and long traditions of open field farming, into parts of Essex where, modern

barley barons permitting, there are still old fields with thick, winding hedgerows, sunken lanes engraved into the setting by the feet of countless generations of travellers, many small and ancient woods and a pattern of settlement which is dominated by scattered hamlets and farmsteads. In much of Devon and the counties of the Welsh Marches the ancient countrysides are also found.

The new form of farming failed to expand across much of England and it is significant that, in places where it was unable to gain a strong foothold, the hamlet and farmstead rather than the village remained as the abodes of most peasants. The explanation for the division of England between areas of open field or 'champion' countryside, which were rich in villages, and of ancient countryside, which were not, remains elusive. Perhaps it may have something to do with the ways in which the old Roman estates had fragmented, for open field farming could only be introduced on estates large enough to encompass a full range of ploughland, meadow and common pasture.

The first steps in the making of village England coincided with the reconversion to Christianity. At first the organization of worship was centred on minster churches. These were staffed by a small community of monks who walked out into the surrounding countryside to conduct services in the open, often at places already hallowed by the pagan religions. Some of these minsters may have been sited in existing settlements, while others were placed at the headquarters of royal estates, as at Fawsley in Northamptonshire, the kings welcoming the recording services offered by literate clerics. One of the best preserved of Saxon churches, almost certainly a minster, is the one at Wing in Buckinghamshire, while one of the most spectacular settings is at Reculver in Kent. Here the church was built inside a Roman fort of the Saxon shore and was later redeveloped with twin towers in Norman times.

Around the tenth century the local lords very frequently built churches for their own use. The Saxon church at Earls Barton in Northamptonshire may have been of this kind. It was placed on a spur guarded by prehistoric earthworks and the original church consisted of little more than a great tower, which may have been used as both a lordly residence and a nave – so that to go to church the thane would simply go downstairs. Churches which began as private chapels for the nobility were opened to congregations composed of local tenants, while new churches were increasingly provided to serve the populations of estates. In this way the estate – a territory which might date back to Roman or even earlier times – became the parish. In some cases the churches were placed in isolated positions, at spots which had experienced both Roman and early Saxon settlement, like Rivenhall, or sites sacred to the old religions. One of the best examples is Rudston in Humberside, where the church stands beside a great monolith, the tallest in Britain, which was probably erected early in Bronze Age times. Most commonly, however, church, manor house and village stood together.

This leaves us to wonder whether villages were attracted to the sites of existing churches or whether churches were provided to serve

The first village churches, the nuclei of most medieval villages, were often minsters, staffed by communities of monks. Wing, in Buckinghamshire, still preserves its Saxon apse, although the rest of the church bears witness to successive rebuildings up to the fifteenth century.

Reculver, in Kent, was an important centre of Saxon Christianity; its early plan survives, but its most prominent features, the twin west towers, are Norman. It was built inside a ruined Roman fort of the Saxon shore.

The Saxon minster at Breamore, near Fordingbridge. Though the doorways are Norman, it appears much as it did when built, around 1000.

the needs of existing villages. There is no all-embracing answer. The great majority of churches were built by local landowners, some before their villages, some after and, quite probably, some at the same time.

There is little cause to suppose that the original form of a village need bear much resemblance to the layout which exists there today. The most thoroughly excavated deserted medieval village, Wharram Percy in Yorkshire, is a good example of this point. There was some settlement here in the Iron Age. During the Roman period four small settlements existed and these may have merged in a single large estate at the end of the era. Interestingly, one lay beneath the site of the later church and one in an enclosure reused by the thirteenth-century manor house. After the Roman era the site was deserted for several centuries, but around the seventh or eighth century new settlers established themselves here. They created not one village but two. One was in the vicinity of the spot where a timber church was erected in the ninth century and the other more than 300 yards (about 300 metres) away to the north-east, in the area of the manor already mentioned. Over the course of several medieval centuries these original villages grew together and merged. The village that resulted, consisting mainly of homesteads strung along the western side of a street or track running from church to manor, had a deceptively coherent appearance which masked the complexity of its real origins.

There are scores of other villages which can be shown to be the products of a growing together of two, three or more formerly quite distinct components. The original components may be smaller villages, hamlets, manors, house clusters around churches or monastic buildings.

Goltho in Lincolnshire is another carefully excavated former village. As at Wharram, there was Roman settlement on the site, but it was deserted in the fourth century. Here too there was a recolonization in the eighth century, when a little village was set out along a road which was later abandoned. With its timber homesteads set in fenced paddocks or gardens, this place must have resembled the villages of the preceding centuries. Around 900, however, the old dwellings were removed and the site which would accommodate the medieval manor house was redeveloped. The new Goltho emerged as a village with a completely different plan and a more typically medieval appearance, with dwellings lining the sides of a high street and side road. This layout survived until Goltho was deserted around 1400. Had Goltho not been abandoned and then been the subject of a rescue excavation about five and a half centuries later, there would have been no obvious reason to imagine that its layout was not the one created by its Saxon founding fathers.

Not only did villages change their layouts, they also embarked upon cross-country migrations. We know this from the evidence of 'field walking'. This technique demands skill, patience and a sturdy pair of legs; the experts systematically walk over ploughed land looking for sherds of pottery. In former times there were no dustbins or refuse collections, while pottery was much more important to each household than it is today. When pots were broken, the sherds were either trampled into the rushes and earth on the floor of the hovel or else they were dumped on the midden outside. Fragments on the midden were spread fairly evenly across the fields in the course of manuring, but those in the floor remained long after the house had gone. Any dense spread of pot fragments denotes a former settlement, while experts can recognize the pots produced by different peoples at different times. A place yielding sherds of red Roman Samian ware and speckled shell-tempered ware of the thirteenth century could have been the site of both a Roman villa and a medieval farmstead.

Long after a settlement has been deserted, the thatch and timber of the dwelling have decayed and the plough has scoured away every little landmark, the diagnostic pottery will remain in the ploughsoil. Field walking has been used to trace the way in which villages have drifted away from their original settings. Peter Wade-Martins has applied this technique to a number of Norfolk villages. One example is Longham. Here the pottery shows that a middle-Saxon village was situated by the parish church and expanded in later Saxon times. In the twelfth century, however, the villagers migrated to a new site around a green which was some distance away to the south and here the medieval village developed. At the end of the Middle Ages Longham was on the move again and the community migrated north-eastwards across their fields to take residence around a common.

The reasons for such drifts are seldom known. In Saxon times villagers might have quit their homes in order to plough the rich soils which had accumulated around their garden plots and middens. In the Middle Ages communities that suffered from a shortage of valuable grazing land could have migrated to live beside pastures or commons, which could then have become large village greens. Not all the moves may have been been voluntary. During the supposedly more civilized centuries that followed the Middle Ages, it was quite common for villages to be uprooted and their communities cast out in order that a stately home could be surrounded by a fashionable uninhabited expanse of open parkland. Medieval lords did not have any scruples about evicting whole communities if it suited them. Villagers might be shifted to clear ground for fishponds or a deer park, resettled at a place with better market trading opportunities or removed from the precincts of an abbey. Burwell in Cambridgeshire is a village which expanded northwards from its middle-Saxon nucleus over a period of six centuries until the elongated village was about a mile and a half in length, but in the course of the building of castle earthworks in 1144 part of the village, which had been settled since the ninth century, was depopulated and destroyed. The outlines of the gardens used by the evicted Norman villagers can still be seen up to the points where they are obliterated by the moat and spoil heaps of the unfinished castle.

Village England, therefore, did not appear suddenly but in the course of several centuries. Once a village had been founded, a dozen or more generations of villagers might come and go before the settlement coalesced into its final shape. Most of the early villages were quite small and often several such places would merge to form one substantial village. Meanwhile, there could be growth in one direction and decay in another. It is not the stability of the English village which impresses so much as its vitality and vulnerability.

Villages vary enormously, but they all have names. Sometimes names that are centuries old have obvious meanings today, like Ashford in Kent, the ford by the ash trees. Frequently the names have little significance today but were plainly meaningful at the times when they were given, like Quorndon in Leicestershire, which was the hill where the quern stones or milling stones were quarried.

Before the archaeologists were able to shed light on the origins of villages, the main source of evidence was provided by place-names. The place-name clues were explored and debated until a most elaborate and seemingly logical explanation was constructed. It was maintained that some place-names dated from the early stages in the Saxon colonization of the wildwood. They included those with the elements 'ham' and 'ton', both relating to settlements; names containing 'ing', which derived from the Old English 'ingas' meaning 'the folk or followers of . . .', and personal names, which identified the founding fathers or patriarchs of the Saxon settlement. Frequently these elements all occurred together, as in Wokingham in Berkshire, 'the homestead of Wocc's folk', or Harrington, Cumbria, 'the farm of Haefer's folk'.

These explanations were founded on a perception of Dark Age English history which seems increasingly more like a mirage than a vision. It imagines victorious Saxon bands following their petty chieftains into the wooded wilderness and establishing primary villages. As these villages filled, it was claimed, so secondary villages were budded off as new farmlands were claimed from the wildwood. These second-generation Saxon villages often had names which included elements like 'ley', from 'leah', a clearing, or ones like 'stock', 'stow' and 'stead', which refer to places of different kinds. Then of course there were the Norse and Danish elements dating from the Viking settlement, like 'by', a farm, 'thorpe', a place or hamlet and 'thwaite', a field or clearing. From time to time the place-names version of history was revised, so that it came to be argued that the oldest of the Saxon names were those that described topographical features. However, during the 1970s and '80s it became clear that the mounting information from recent archaeological surveys and excavations was painting a very different picture and that the place-name evidence itself could be used to argue a different case.

Take, for example, the 'ham' and 'ton' names which were supposed to reveal early Saxon villages. Most frequently the old English 'ham' described not a village but a homestead. In some places it is actually combined with the 'stead' word, for example 'hamstede', to produce the various Hampstead and Hamsted place-names. Neither does the Old English 'tun' describe a village, but rather a farm or an enclosure – and it was still being used in this way until after the Norman Conquest. Royston in Hertfordshire developed as a medieval town and was initially named after a cross at the intersection of the ancient Icknield Way and the Roman Ermine Street; in 1184 the village was called Crux Roasie, meaning Rohesia's Cross, and it was not until a century later that its name became Royston. There are also problems with other important clues, like the word 'ley', which was supposed to reveal clearings made by colonists from the first generation of villages. Field walking has shown that names ending in 'ley' occur in places which were not Dark Age woodland but which have existed as working farmland continuously since prehistoric times. In such places 'ley' may describe not clearings but the reverse, small groups of trees preserved because they were in short supply and useful.

The Norman interior of the important Saxon minster church at Stow, near Lincoln. Like many other minster churches, Stow has a cruciform plan.

The misleading nature of place-name evidence has been demonstrated by the archaeologist Christopher Taylor, in relation to archaeological work carried out by Dr L. Butler at Faxton in Northamptonshire, a village which declined and gradually disappeared

in the 1950s. The name Faxton was translated as 'the farm of the Viking, Fakr', giving the impression that it was created during the Danish settlement of the East Midlands in the decades around 800. It certainly seemed to have prospered by 1086, when Domesday Book recorded twenty-one heads of peasant households on the Faxton manor. Nevertheless, the archaeological survey showed that, in fact, there was no settlement here before 1150 and that the village was not deliberately set out as a coherent whole until 1200.

Now we can offer an interpretation of the evidence which seems much more convincing. In the course of the several centuries on either side of the Norman conquest, settlement was gravitating from farmstead and hamlet to new villages. The villages had one or several nuclei and the most common of these focal points must have been existing homesteads and farmsteads, places that already had names. As the new villages coalesced, they took over the names of the older settlements. In this way the numerous Dentons have a name meaning 'valley farm', the Duddingtons and Doddingtons were all farms belonging to the folk of men called 'Dudda', Bloxham in Oxfordshire was Blocc's homestead, just as Amersham in Buckinghamshire was that of Ealhmund. Of course, these names tell us nothing about the actual ages of the villages that duly inherited them. There is no way of telling if people like Dudda, Blocc and Ealhmund were in fact the founders of the farmsteads and homesteads bearing their names or else patriarchs or figures of authority who emerged later. Nor can we know when the nuclei provided by farmsteads and hamlets were expanded to become villages.

Place-name evidence is still of real value and it can tell us something about the history of the English village – but something of a less direct kind. Quite often the names tell us about the old settings in which the villages developed. Barton Bendish in Norfolk was 'the grain farm which lies within the (ancient earthwork known as the Devil's Ditch) dyke'; Pinchbeck in Lincolnshire was by the stream of the finches; Tackley in Oxfordshire was the place where the young sheep grazed; and Hemsted in Kent was where hemp was grown. Sometimes the names tell us about people who influenced the local settlement history: Mevagissey in Cornwall was at the site of a church dedicated to the saints Mews and Ida; the Barnet villages which were overrun by London were named after a burnt place; Chipping Barnet was the Barnet which had a market and, as well as High, East and New Barnet, there was also Friern Barnet, the holders being not friars but members of the Knights of St John of Jerusalem. More common are the numerous Knighton villages, some of them associated with manors held by the Knights Templars.

Early medieval villagers were obsessed with the Domesday or Last Judgment. Here the theme is illustrated by the head of the splendidly carved Norman doorway at Barfrestone in Kent.

In 1085, almost twenty years after the conquest of England, William I held his Christmas court at Gloucester. It was here that he engaged in deep thought about a survey of his realm, one which proved to be so penetrating and pervasive that the English would associate it with the Last Judgment and call it 'Domesday'. In awe and apprehension the author of the entry in the Anglo-Saxon Chronicle reported that: 'He sent his men all over England into every shire and had them find out how many hundred hides there were in the shire . . . So very narrowly did he have it investigated, that there was no single hide nor a yard of land, nor indeed (it is a shame to relate but it seemed no shame to him to do) one ox nor one cow nor one pig which was there left out, and not put in his records: and all these records were brought to him afterwards.'

In fact, the Saxon cleric was being unduly pessimistic, for even in the English heartlands the surveyors were often capable of overlooking churches, their priests and profitable watermills. Even so, the investigations were far more comprehensive than anything which had been known before and only the medieval and modern poll taxes have caused such consternation in the countryside.

Soon after the survey Robert, bishop of Hereford, explained how the task had been accomplished. The king's servants had 'made a survey of all England; of the lands in each of the counties; of the possessions of each of the magnates, their lands, their habitations, their men both bond and free, living in huts or with their own houses and lands; of ploughs, horses, and other animals; of the services and payments due from each and every estate'.

*Above: the Saxon tower
of Earls Barton, in
Northamptonshire.*

*Right: the medieval
church beside the Bronze
Age monolith at
Rudston.*

Following the initial survey other investigators were despatched to check the data gathered and report on any malpractices, according to Bishop Robert. 'And the land was troubled with many calamities arising from the gathering of the royal taxes.'

The records of the Abbey of Ely provide a near-contemporary description of the way in which the material was gathered:

Here follows an inquiry concerning the lands which the king's barons made according to the oath of the sheriff of the shire and of all the barons and their Frenchmen, and of the whole hundred court – the priests, reeves and six villeins from each village. They inquired what the manor was called; who held it in the time of King Edward [the Confessor]; who holds it now; how many hides there are; how many ploughs in demesne and how many belonging to the men; how many villeins; how many cottars; how many slaves; how many free men; how many sokemen; how much woodland; how much meadow; how much pasture; how many mills; how many fisheries; how much has been added to, or taken away from, the estate; what it used to be worth then [in King Edward's time]; what it is worth now, and how much each freeman and sokeman had or has . . .

Not all the actual entries are as comprehensive as this implies and in the more marginal and troubled parts of the kingdom they are very much abbreviated. The information was set down in a sort of standardized Latin shorthand on vellum pages. These were later bound to produce Great Domesday Book and the more detailed Little Domesday, which covered the final returns for the eastern circuit counties of Essex, Suffolk and Norfolk. Despite the economical style and pruning of the entries, Great Domesday has 413 vellum leaves, produced from the skins of between 500 and 1000 small sheep, and Little Domesday has 475 leaves. This sample entry for Washingley in Huntingdonshire shows the concise manner in which the information was recorded:

In Washingley Ketelbert had 2½ taxable hides [a hide was about 120 acres/ 50 hectares]. Land for 4 ploughs. He now holds of the king and has there 1 plough and 10 villeins with 4 ploughs. There is a church there and a priest; and 12 acres of meadow; and woodland pasture, 7 furlongs in length, 10½ in width. In the time of King Edward and now is worth 10 shillings.

To understand Domesday Book, we must remember that it was compiled to the commands of King William I, who was a ruthless pragmatist. He had risen from a relatively obscure and extremely unstable background to secure the dukedom of Normandy and had then, by dint of great good fortune and remarkable determination, fulfilled his highest ambition – the right to wear a king's crown. William was not a popular man and certainly not loved by the Saxon monks who compiled their historical chronicle, but when William died in 1087, a year after the completion of his great survey, the chronicle left a fair account of the man. He was 'a very wise man, and very powerful and more worshipful and stronger than any of his predecessors had been. He was gentle to the good men who loved God, and stern beyond all measure to those people who resisted his will . . . The good security he made in this country is not to be forgotten, so that any honest man could travel over his kingdom with his bosom full of gold: and no man dare strike another, no matter how much wrong he had done him.'

William's insistence on a firm and thoroughgoing administration was combined with an avaricious nature and an intuitive grasp of politics and economics. His character and experience led him to realize the advantages of assessing all his taxable assets and of binding all his vassals tightly into a feudal system which eliminated any scope for dispute. All these factors combined to produce Domesday Book. Contrary to latterday popular myth, William was not interested in recording history. His overriding interest was encapsulated by Bishop Robert; it was to make 'a survey of all . . . the services and payments due from each and every estate'.

Domesday Book was a survey of estates or manors. Neither William nor his inquisitors showed the remotest interest in villages. For all that they cared the peasants could have been living in villages, up trees or in pits in the ground. All that mattered was that the servile people should create the wealth of the kingdom and that the king's tenants who prospered from it should render full rents and services for the estates that they held of the king. The most common misconception about Domesday Book is based on the idea that it is a survey of villages. In fact, the places named are *not* villages but estates.

Researches, like field walking, have shown that some of these estates contained no villages at all, while others could embrace a clutch of villages, farmsteads and hamlets. Many of the villages were still in the process of amalgamating from the merger of several different settlement nuclei. An example is my native village, mentioned in Domesday Book as 'Beristade'. All the documentation possible exists to prove that there was no village of Birstwith until the nineteenth century, when an estate village was created by the millowners-turned-squires of the Greenwood family. The place mentioned in Domesday Book is not a village but a communal locality or 'township'. The appearance of a village's name in Domesday is no proof of its existence in 1086, for it seems that as villages formed they took over the names of estates as well as of

Overleaf:
The ruined church at the deserted medieval village of Wharram Percy in Yorkshire.

55

farms, much as did the parishes which were so often based on older estates.

Domesday Book's real value is as a source of information about the early days of the English village. It tells us nothing about the existence, appearance or layout of the villages through which the inquisitors trekked. But it does tell us a great deal about the village setting. It also gives an impression of the numbers of the different peasant classes, many members of which were villagers.

By the time of Domesday, the framework of the English countryside had been established. Contrary again to later myth, the village settings were seldom well wooded. Perhaps about one eighth of the realm was wooded and almost all the woodland was managed and exploited for fuel and working timber. Much of this woodland existed in a form seldom seen today – wood pasture, where livestock grazed beneath the spreading boughs of the pollarded trees. More than a third of the countryside was ploughland and Domesday records some 81,000 ploughs, while about a quarter of land was pasture – much of it needed to support the one million oxen, cows and calves associated with the ploughing industry. Extra grazing was found on commons with moorland, heath and marsh, and in such places most of the kingdom's two million sheep would have been found. The weakness in the arsenal of Domesday village farming seems to have been a shortage of meadow land, for hay was vital to sustain livestock through the harsh winter months.

Domesday village society was feudal and slashed apart by class divisions, which not only separated man from master, but which also divided toiler from toiler. The survey only listed the heads of households. The kingdom's landlords, priests, petty landowners and free peasants were outnumbered by a factor of more than five to one by a great mass of about 225,000 bond peasants (since the inquisitors were capable of overlooking the odd castle, let alone many mills and churches, it is safe to guess that this is a considerable underestimate). If, as the authorities generally allow, the heads of households were the heads of families averaging five members each, and if many folk were not recorded, then the population of Domesday England would have been somewhere above three million.

We know that the village communities were riven with class distinctions, but it is not easy to unravel all the complexities. Domesday Book illustrates how the new Norman masters attempted to apply their values to the captive English society. Unlike the English, they did not deal in outright slavery, but they made a distinction between free tenants and bondsmen or serfs. In Domesday Book the most numerous of the bond tenants are classed as 'villeins' but there are also many listings of 'bordars', who had a more lowly status. This continental image of society was superimposed on English village communities, in which the class divisions were more complicated and ambiguous.

Saxon England was still a slave-owning society, although slavery had declined after the disruptions of the Viking wars, when many slaves had been freed. Freedom was given partly as an act of Christian goodwill and partly to relieve the masters of the burden of supporting slaves, who might prove more economical as self-supporting bond tenants. Sometimes the act of freeing a slave was performed at a crossroads, showing that the fortunate man or woman was now free to leave in any direction. Villagers just above the status of slaves were 'cotsetlan' or cottagers, who rented small-holdings and managed to subsist by working for modest wages on their free days. The backbone of the servile village workforce was composed of tenants of the 'gebur' rank, and the broader class of churls included cottagers, geburs and men of 'gafolgelda' status, who were rent-paying tenants. Were a gebur to be called a slave, he would probably have been offended beyond measure, yet his status was so wretched that the only difference between his condition and slavery was the fact that his lord did not have the right to whip him. When manors were sold, a few churls could be thrown in almost as an afterthought.

Standing apart from the ranks of the bondsmen was the free tenant or 'geneat'. He was still liable to pay rent and render services for his lord, although the work was generally less arduous and unpleasant and often involved being a horseman or riding errands. As a free tenant, he had the right, if he were accused of a crime, to be tried at a royal court and thus escape the tyranny of the manor court. However, the realities of the situation were still more complicated than those outlined here. For example, status was connected with land as well as households, so that a servile bordar could tenant some land associated with free service, while a starving cottar or cottager could be a free man and a large and prosperous holding could be tenanted by a serf-like bordar.

The Domesday village community was bowed down by burdensome obligations. The Normans may have refined feudalism and shattered the bonds of loyalty which bound the churls and free peasants to their lords or thanes, but the manors of old Saxon England were entwined in the most intricate webs of obligations. It was recorded that around 1030 on the manor at Hurstbourne Priors in Hampshire

The reasons why villages are born, persist and disappear are always of deep interest. The village of Comberton, in Cambridgeshire, drifted away from its church (right) to exploit a new roadside location.

Ickleton, in Cambridgeshire, is a village of uncertain antiquity, but it sits astride the great prehistoric highway into Wessex known as the Icknield Way.

Opposite: Burwell, on the edge of the Fens, in Cambridgeshire, grew longer and longer throughout the Middle Ages, thriving as a river port served by an ancient canal or 'lode'.

Earl Soham, in Suffolk (right), has a name meaning 'homestead by the lake'. The lake was drained long ago, but Domesday Book proves its former existence. The forename refers to the medieval proprietors, the Earls of Norfolk, to distinguish this village from Monk Soham, owned by the Abbey of Bury St Edmunds.

THE BIRTH OF VILLAGE ENGLAND

each churl tenanting a large holding of about 120 acres had to render the following rents and services:

40 pence at the autumnal equinox, and 6 church 'mittan' of ale and 3 'sesters' [about 3 pint measures] of wheat for bread, and they must plough 3 acres in their own time, and sow them with their own seed, and bring it to the barn in their own time, and give 3 pounds of barley as rent, and mow half an acre of meadow as rent in their own time, and make it into a rick, and supply 4 'fothers' of split wood as rent, made into a stack in their own time, and supply 16 poles of fencing as rent likewise in their own time, and at Easter they shall give 2 ewes and 2 lambs – we reckon 2 young sheep to a full grown sheep – and they must wash the sheep and shear them in their own time, and work as they are bidden every week except three – one at midwinter, the second at Easter, the third at the Rogation Days.

Despite these heavy duties the villager guarded his status with fierce jealousy – and although the manorial system exploited him to the hilt he had great reverence for the ancient customs of the manor. Two of the main causes of violence and disquiet in the villages of Saxon and Domesday England were insults which diminished a man's standing in the community and breaches of hallowed customs. In return for performing a crippling burden of duties, villagers could be entitled to modest privileges. In the reign of Cnut (1016–35) a slave woman was entitled to eight pounds of grain, one sheep or three pennies to sustain her through winter, about a pint of beans at Lent and a grant of whey or one penny in summer, while all slaves enjoyed feasts at Christmas and Easter and an extra handful of grain at harvest. The village shepherd did rather better, for the flock could be pastured to manure his land for twelve nights at Christmas and he could claim one lamb, a fleece and the milk from his flock for seven nights before the autumn equinox and a cup of buttermilk throughout the summer. When we realize how highly these tiny privileges were valued, we can begin to appreciate just how grinding the conditions of village life really were during the childhood of village England.

4 The anatomy of the village

The villages of the Middle Ages, as we have seen, had often coalesced from the merging of several smaller places. But these medieval villages still had, by and large, more coherent layouts than those of earlier ages. The high street, the green, the cottage row and the back lane were all facets of the village landscape which were repeated again and again. Though the villages in the Englands of King Arthur, King Alfred and King Harold remain partly mysterious, those of the Middle Ages are now well known, for scores of deserted medieval villages have been photographed from the air, surveyed or excavated. We can paint a fairly accurate picture of how such places looked, even how they smelled, though there is still much more to be discovered. It is very seldom that the exact origins of a particular village are known and other questions concern topics like the ages and uses made of village greens and the identities of those who set out the village plan. Most modern villagers who take pride in their home place will be keen to discover something about its antiquity. When walking to the village store does one tread in the footsteps of Saxon geburs and medieval villeins? Was the core of the village once centred on the church and has the green been here since the time of Robin Hood?

Information about medieval village planning can sometimes be gathered from old documents but it is most frequently deduced from the fabric of the village itself. Planning is associated with order, with straight streets, right-angled junctions, rectangular property blocks, regularly shaped market areas and plot frontages of standardized widths. Such features in the village anatomy suggest that the village

Castleton, in Derbyshire, seems at first to be a haphazard old village. In fact, it was planned by the owners of its overlooking Norman castle and has a geometrical gridwork of streets and a triangular market green below the church.

had a creator with distinct motives and a geographical plan in mind if not on paper.

Medieval kings and nobles planned towns but the moving forces in village planning were usually the local lords of manors, men who saw an advantage in reorganizing the peasant community or launching a little market. Sometimes entire villages were created but in other cases only a part of an existing village was redeveloped or expanded. Of course if a lord masterminded the creation of a new village but did not bother to prescribe an organized plan, then there may be no clue to reveal the origins of the place. It is very seldom indeed that documents survive to record the origins of a village.

One exception is the village of Bainbridge in Wensleydale. Situated at the foot of a glacial mound, which was formerly crowned by a Roman military outpost, Bainbridge has origins which are revealed in a legal demand of 1227, which required one Ranulph son of Robert to state by what right he had created villages and houses in the forest of Wensleydale. He replied that Bainbridge had been founded by his forbears, who were responsible for the forest, so that a community of twelve foresters could be supported, each forester being provided with a house and nine acres of land. The villages of Buckden in Wharfedale and Healaugh in Swaledale seem to have had similar origins.

A more thoroughly documented example has been described by the noted researcher of village layouts, Brian Roberts, in *The Making of the English Village*. In 1567 a surveyor was composing a record of the estates of the Earl of Northumberland and referred to the manor of Thirston in that county: 'being seytuat together and far from parte of their grounds, was by the scytuacon thereof unprofitable and therefore removed towards Acklington parke to a place moche more comodyous than where it stood'. The old village of West Thirston had been devastated by Scottish raiding in 1324 and was rebuilt in the 1330s. The hiving-off of a part of the population of West Thirston to fill the new village of East Thirston was undertaken to remove the inconveniences caused by long journeys to and from the widely scattered field strips. Though plainly created as a single act of policy, East Thirston has a traditional medieval layout, but it lacks the disciplined geometry which would loudly proclaim its planned origins. There is a roughly 'L-shaped' arrangement of cottage rows flanking a broad street or green.

Several other examples of village relocations are known, like the cases of East Witton in Wensleydale and New Byland on the flanks of the North York Moors. In both cases the villagers were uprooted for the convenience of the Cistercian monks who were their masters.

Two medieval Yorkshire villages. Top: Buckden, in Wharfedale, is a popular tourist village and seems to have been created to house a community of foresters. Bainbridge, in Wensleydale, is one of very few old villages with recorded origins. It was built to provide homes for twelve foresters at the start of the thirteenth century.

Left: the green at Cavendish, in Suffolk, formed after the village coalesced from several medieval hamlets.

Below: East Witton, in Wensleydale, was rebuilt in 1809 but preserves the outlines of the market village built by Jervaulx Abbey five centuries earlier.

Right: buttercups adorn the planned rectangular green at Arncliffe in the Yorkshire Dales.

The green at Eltisley, in Cambridgeshire, scene of the local cricket match, can be traced back to Saxon times when the village was first laid out.

During the late thirteenth century the monks of Jervaulx Abbey increased their control of the East Witton estates and the forced removal of the village to a site where its intrusion on the solitude of the monastery was much less probably occurred around 1307. It was then that permission was granted for a cattle fair and weekly market, presumably as valuable assets for the new village. Although the houses of East Witton were rebuilt in stone by the Earl of Ailesbury in 1809 to mark the jubilee of George III, the village layout was scarcely affected and the typical medieval plan of an elongated green flanked on either side by rows of cottages still survives.

The Byland Abbey community originally settled in Ryedale in a place so close to Rievaulx Abbey that the ringing of two sets of bells caused confusion. The shift to the new Byland site followed, but the first abbey site had already been cleared by the enforced removal of a population of villagers. They were transplanted to a new site more than a mile away and the monks provided them with a stone church. The twelfth-century layout of Old Byland still survives remarkably well and the village has never grown very much: houses face each other across a broad, rectangular green.

Planned villages can be found throughout the British Isles and they were created at all periods from the Norman to the modern. Some could be older still and Christopher Taylor suggests Creaton in Northamptonshire and Eltisley in Cambridgeshire as examples of planned villages with greens which were set out in Saxon times. The greatest concentration is found in the Vale of York and its adjacent areas. This was the part of England which bore the brunt of the ghastly Harrying of the North in 1069–71, when the Conqueror's host was unleashed in a campaign of genocide against the recalcitrant folk of Yorkshire and Durham. It is hard to imagine that the multitude of planned villages here did not originate from an organized revitalization of the local manors in the aftermath of the killings and burnings. A favoured type of layout, surviving in many places to this day, involved lining the sides of a through road with long, narrow house plots which ran back from this road. The dwellings were placed in line close to the roadside. Sometimes the road was broadened as it passed through the village to create a green and often the ends of the plots furthest from the road were defined by back lanes.

In some carefully investigated Yorkshire villages there is evidence that the dimensions of the plots were precisely measured. Records dating from the start of the twelfth century show that the townlet of Battle in Sussex had already been 'laid out with fixed measurements of house plots'. The abbey at Battle was built on land granted by King William I and its high altar was placed over the spot where King Harold's standard was believed to have flown at the battle of Hastings. The new settlement was erected just outside the abbey gates, with members of the abbey community supervising the delimitation of the plots.

There are several reasons why so many English villages became the calculated creations of local magnates. In the cases of countrysides devastated by civil strife or Scottish invasion, the lords of the local manors had every reason to get their estates back into productive work – and the creation of settlements for the peasant workforces must have ranked high in the calculations for recovery. Practical considerations also made it sensible to establish new peasant dormitories on lands which lay inconveniently distant from the mother village. Meanwhile, the provision of new homes for folk evicted by Cistercian expansion was a price which some monks chose to pay. Markets also exerted an influence, for the lord who had successfully petitioned for a market charter could expect a steady trickle of income to accrue from market tolls and fines. Between the start of the thirteenth century and the middle of the fourteenth century around 2000 new markets were chartered.

If the village was designated as a market centre but tended to be bypassed by traders and customers, then it seemed sensible to move it to a more lively setting. In such a way Caxton in Cambridgeshire left its church behind and took a new position astride the Great North Road when a market charter was gained in the middle of the thirteenth century. A planned market-place formed the centrepiece of the new village.

In some cases, like East Witton or Milburn in Cumbria, the planned medieval layouts survive much as their makers intended. Milburn seems to have been redeveloped after the Norman period, for its Norman church was left stranded when the village was shifted

Left: Wensley from the north, showing the green in the foreground

Below: though the weekly markets at Masham, North Yorkshire, are almost extinct, the great annual sheep fair still fills the vast market square at the start of autumn.

Right: the cross at Hardingstone, Northamptonshire, is most unusual, one of a small series of crosses erected by Edward I at the places where the coffin of Queen Eleanor had rested overnight en route for burial at London.

and rebuilt around a rectangular green. In other cases later growth has masked the original geometric order, as at Thriplow in Cambridgeshire. There are also villages where a planned section of development was inserted into an older settlement. Often this would occur when a village gained a market, as at Sheriff Hutton in North Yorkshire, which acquired a market in 1378 and a castle four years later.

The most evocative part of the village landscape is the green. Greens are areas of common grassland which lie within the village boundaries – but it is impossible to construct a fuller definition because they vary so enormously. They can be enormous expanses of grassland, such as those at Barrington in Cambridgeshire or Long Melford in Suffolk. They can be narrow ribbons of grass, like those which flank the through roads at so many of the northern planned villages. Or they can be neat rectangles, like the ones at Milburn or Arncliffe in the Yorkshire Dales. In addition to the rectangles there are also triangles, patches, broadenings of streets and villages with several greens. And then there are the greens obliterated, distorted or reduced by later developments.

When we bear all these variations in mind, it is impossible to believe that village greens had a common origin or identical sorts of use. Old documents do not contain much information and most of our understanding has to be inferred or deduced. And so it would be easy to make mistakes; my own village shows how such mistakes could be made. Between the vicarage and the post office the roads widen at a 'T'-junction – and at a similar junction in the very next village, Hampsthwaite, there is a triangular green which was almost certainly created to accommodate a fourteenth-century market. In Birstwith, however, the 'green' originated in the nineteenth century as an attractive landscaping feature known locally as 'The Plantpot'; at the junction one road forked to embrace a cluster of elm trees surrounded by a low stone wall. Around 1950 the authorities, with characteristic thoughtlessness, chose to fell the elms and replace them with an expanse of grass. Another outbreak of thoughtlessness removed the wall. Newcomers to the village then labelled this 'the green' and so it remained until 1990, when a further incident of official vandalism reduced the green to a mere roundabout, enabling the heavy lorries which had battered the edges of the 'green' to traverse the village at even more frightening speeds. Most greens are centuries old but few have survived unaltered; some were always tiny patches of grass but many have been trimmed and nibbled and encroached upon until they are reduced to nothing.

Some large greens must have originated as commons. There is a long tradition of settlement around the edges of commons which continued to Victorian times. The poorest members of a community might enjoy no more than the right to pasture a few animals on a common and for such folk, and for more affluent people too, there was an advantage in being able to put beasts out directly on to a patch of shared grazing. As settlement gravitated towards a common, so a village grew from the straggle of farmsteads and squatter cottages along the common edge. Such growth might surround a small common, affect just one side of it or line the side of an access road to create a village shaped like a tadpole, with the green forming the head and the dwellings lining the lane that was the tail. Patches of trackside common were magnets for settlement when the population grew rapidly in the twelfth and thirteenth centuries. The results of this development are the rather straggling or formless hamlets and small villages so abundant in East Anglia and the East Midlands and frequently known by the names 'Green' or 'End', like Hall Green and Wood End near Stevenage. Very few of these places ever managed to grow to the size of a respectable village. Today many are reduced to just a few cottages and farmsteads, though the traces of former house sites can often be recognized. In Norfolk, a county littered with decayed medieval settlement, ancient commons seem to have had a special magnetism and stranded churches and deserted house sites pattern the edges of many greens.

Other greens were so compact and so thoroughly integrated with the village layout that they can never have originated in this way. Some must have been part and parcel of the process of village making, as at Nun Monkton in North Yorkshire, where the rows of dwellings of this former river port and ecclesiastical centre were set out neatly around a large triangular green. But greens could also be inserted into the layout of a village which already existed. The most likely occasion for this would have been when the lord gained a market charter. With the prospect of a respectable income from tolls and fines, the lord would not let the existence of a handful of inconveniently placed peasant hovels stand in his way. If the village already had a green which could accommodate the new market, all well and good, but if not, then either the market would be built on a plot near existing dwellings or houses would be torn down to clear a market-place. Christopher Taylor discovered one of the most interesting cases, that of Culworth and Brime in Northamptonshire. These existed as two separate but adjacent villages until 1264, when the local lord gained the right to hold a market. He had a square market-place inserted between the villages and properties were

The guildhall at the fossilized medieval town at Thaxted, Essex, was built for the local guild of cutlers.

The village pond at Newton-on-Rawcliffe, Yorkshire (right), may, like the village, be a Norman creation.

Wensley's large church proclaims the prosperity it enjoyed before the plague struck in 1563. It never recovered and is now only a small village.

established around it. This growth formed a bridge between the settlements and Culworth and Brime became one.

The average medieval village market was a humdrum place where the most exotic and enticing wares displayed might be blocks of salt or bags of nails. Fairs were much more entertaining, being visited by itinerant traders from far afield with colourful cloth, sparkling metalware, pungent spices and all manner of wholesale goods. The typical market grant specified a weekly market, to be held on a day chosen so as not to clash with other village markets in the neighbourhood, and an annual fair, frequently specified for the day of the patron saint of the village church. Sometimes market and fair were held at the same venue, though the most successful fairs covered a large area and were held on the outskirts of towns or villages or on open sites. At Higham in Norfolk there was a rectangular market-place, lined all around by dwellings and shops, and a triangular 'Fair Land' on the southern outskirts of the village.

In the twelfth and thirteenth centuries, when English trade was buoyant, markets erupted throughout the countryside. There was money to be made, or so it seemed, and the speculators were many. However, once a lord had bought his market grant, he found that his village was in competition with all the other villages in the locality. Few village markets really prospered. Most staggered along for a few centuries, some still stagger, but many had withered away before the Middle Ages had passed. Sometimes the baton of leadership was passed to and fro as outbreaks of pestilence, rises and falls in the patronage of local trade routes and fluctuations in local entrepreneurship all affected the issue.

Wensleydale takes its name from Wensley, an attractive little village today, but scarcely the sort of place that one would name things after. In 1306 Wensley gained its market and prospered, but in 1563 the Black Death struck both Wensley and the market centre of East Witton on the other side of the river Ure. Wensley never recovered its vitality and lost its trade to Askrigg, further up the dale, which was granted a market and two fairs in 1587. Askrigg's commercial leadership lasted little more than a century, for in 1699 Hawes obtained a market charter, eroded the trade of its rival, and Askrigg market dwindled away completely at the start of the nineteenth century. In the meantime other hopeful but essentially hopeless markets had appeared in this economic backwater, at places like Carperby, where a mere broadening of the village through road to form a tiny trading triangle and a cross dated 1634 reflect the ambitions of former days.

The existence of markets and the original uses made of village greens may be forgotten but greens and markets seldom disappear without leaving a permanent mark upon the layout of a village. Sometimes relics of the medieval cross, provided to mark and bless

Sometimes early Christian relics – like this Celtic cross in the churchyard at Altarnun in Cornwall – provide hints of the antiquity of worship and settlement.

The early seventeenth-century market cross at Carperby, more a symbol of hope than glory.

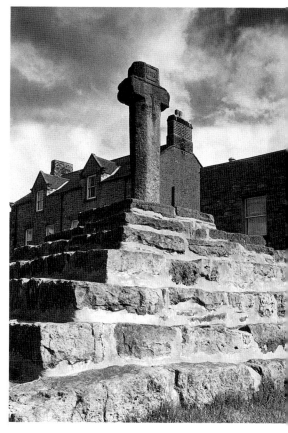

Right: at Ripley, near Harrogate, this road, of perhaps a Roman vintage, formed the village axis until the village was replanned early in the nineteenth century. Here it runs past the castle gates towards the market square.

Below: at Burnsall, in Wharfedale, the village seems to have grown from its old hillside church nucleus towards a crossing place on the Wharfe.

Opposite: the Saxon church at Beechamwell, in Norfolk, is the sole survivor of the three churches needed to serve the medieval village.

the market, survive. Seldom cruciform in shape, these crosses often consisted of stone shafts standing on stepped plinths and supporting lantern-shaped heads. A few remain almost intact, as at Ripley near Harrogate, where there are stocks at the base of the plinth. More often one may find fragments of the plinth or a stumpy cross shaft, the remainder having been demolished in the days when all crosses were attacked as 'popish symbols'. In more prosperous places more elaborate roofed or vaulted crosses were built, like the butter cross at the cheese-making village of Cheddar in Somerset which sheltered the old market cross.

It is much more unusual to find an old market house still standing. Such buildings, which vary in design but which often date from the later stages of the Middle Ages, were used to house the components of booths, stalls and pens on the six non-trading days of the week. These were stored at ground level, while on the floor above there was the chamber used as the venue for the court of 'pie powder', where the local trading regulations were enforced (the strange name derived from a French term describing the dusty feet of traders arriving via rutted lanes). At Winster in Derbyshire, formerly a market town, a market house survives to commemorate the commerce. Originally it had a ground-floor level of stonework pierced by broad arches and an upper level in timber-framing, but the arches are blocked and the storey above was rebuilt in brick around 1675.

On the green at Elstow in Bedfordshire there is a very fine market house in timber-framing with brick infill panels which dates from about 1500. Guildhalls are old public buildings which might be mistaken for market houses. In villages which are really declined trading towns they were sometimes built by local craft guilds – there is no better example than the guildhall built for the cutlers of Thaxted in Essex around 1420. Other examples, like the one at Whittlesford in Cambridgeshire, were used by friendly societies associated with the local church. The fourteenth-century Court House at Long Crendon in Buckinghamshire has an upper floor which was a staple hall, used to store the wool sheared in the locality prior to its sale.

Very few greens sport maypoles and those that are found are expressions of fairly recent whimsy. One cannot know how common maypoles were, but they seem to have been rare for quite a long time. In 1796 Samuel Taylor Coleridge wrote a very dubious account of the origins of the ritual of maypole dancing and decided that because it involved the villagers in electing a lord or king it symbolized ancient freedoms: 'The May-Pole, then, is the English Tree of Liberty! Are there many yet standing?'

The market house at
Winster, Derbyshire,
which has shrunk from a
market town to a village.
The lower part is
medieval, the upper
storey of about 1675.

Where greens have been lost, their departure could be gradual or
sudden. If the lord and the village community tolerated the erection
of squatter cottages on the common land of the green or the
encroachment by bordering properties, then a green could slowly be
reduced or disappear completely. Brian Roberts has explored maps
of Hayton in Cumbria which illustrate these events very well. When
depicted in 1603, the village dwellings lined the sides of an elongated
green, but already tenements and their yards had been established to
form a string of private islands running along the centre of the public
green. When Hayton was mapped again in 1866, all traces of the
green had vanished and half of it was covered in a jumble of tightly
packed dwellings. As areas of common land, village greens were
vulnerable to privatization under the Parliamentary Enclosure
legislation of the eighteenth and nineteenth centuries. Such enclosures
were highly unpopular and the new act passed in 1845 attempted to
put a stop to them. The greens so affected could be parcelled out
between bordering properties or could, as G. K. Chesterton
mentioned, turn up in the squire's backyard. It was normal for
village dwellings to face directly on to a green or the road which
bordered it. Where old dwellings lining a village road have front

gardens, it is more than likely that the gardens have been carved from a former green. One of the best examples is Cold Kirby in North Yorkshire, where the stone-walled front gardens of the Norman-planned village result from the enclosure of a rectangular green early in the nineteenth century.

Greens could be useful as pastures or as market-places. It is not always easy to know just why particular greens were created, but the length of their survival suggests they must have been useful. Cattle could have been turned out, after sleeping close to their owners in the village hovels, to assemble on a green and await the call of the cow herd; ducks and geese could graze safely on the common pasture overlooked by cottages and the green was always available for sports on the feast days which enlivened the village year. The least credible explanation of the existence of village greens is the one which was the most popular: that greens were defensive enclosures for livestock. In a small number of northern villages affected by Scottish raids this interpretation might in fact be justified – though evidence shows that in times of danger villagers had the good sense to let their beasts loose in the woods. There is not a shred of evidence to show that the Saxon settlers corralled their cattle at night on greens protected by a ring of dwellings.

Some villages had ponds or greens containing ponds. Occasionally the pond may have been the initial magnet for settlement. Ashmore, high on the dry chalk uplands of Cranborne Chase in Dorset, has a large embanked pond which may have existed since Roman times, allowing settlement to flourish within a parched setting. There are other ponds which could easily be as old as the village which surrounds them. One of the most spectacular is the circular, man-made pool on the otherwise parched slope of the North York Moors at Newton-on-Rawcliffe, a settlement which may date from early Norman times. Other ponds seen in or close to villages had more specialized uses. Some served village mills, like the Saxon and medieval mill pond excavated and cleared at Wharram Percy.

Fishponds were provided to serve the needs of the lord of the manor rather than the villagers. They were artificial and shallow, outlined by earthbanks which were breached here and there by the sluice gates used to regulate the flow. Often several ponds of increasing size were set in line, with young fish being moved along the chain of ponds until they reached the main one and were ready to be netted. Such ponds can often be recognized as earthworks on the outskirts of a village or at deserted village sites. There is a good example at Cublington. Usually they lay close to the manor house so

The ancient village pond at Ashmore, Dorset.

that the lord and his retainers could keep an eye on poachers. Sometimes the waters from the manor house moat were then diverted to serve a mill or fishpond complex.

Villages always needed a water supply and this could be provided by a spring, a stream – which invariably became more foul as it followed its course through the dwellings – or by a well. As standards of hygiene gradually rose, so village pumps were superseded by piped supplies, polluted wells were sealed, while tainted streams were culverted. The degree to which a source of water attracted settlement must have depended upon the widespread availability or otherwise of such supplies. In some cases villages grew beside springs and wells which had been sacred in pagan times and which were often rededicated to a more acceptable Christian saint – and so became holy wells. The saints Anne, Agnes and Helen were popular patrons and must frequently have served as substitutes for Celtic deities like Elen and the fearsome Annis. More holy wells lay outside villages than within them, but a properly promoted well could be a useful asset – like the example by the churchyard wall at Stevington in Bedfordshire, which once attracted pilgrims afflicted with diseases of the eyes. Most famous are the Derbyshire wells associated with the custom of well dressing, the five wells at the exceptionally attractive estate village of Tissington and other wells at places like Eyam, Stoney Middleton and Wormhill. At Tissington the tradition has certainly existed since the eighteenth century and some people trace its origins to the mid-fourteenth century. The ceremony takes place on Ascension Day, when the wells are dressed with panels of clay decorated with colourful flowers, leaves and mosses.

The twelfth- and thirteenth-century fortified manor house at Stokesay, in Shropshire, survives exceptionally well, but the associated village was deserted long ago.

Manor houses were frequently situated in villages but they related to estates more than to settlements. There are plenty of villages which lacked these noble residences, known by the old names 'hallgarth' in the north and 'barton' in the south, though many villages had several. In 1086 Harbury in Warwickshire had five manors and two centuries later it had no fewer than two lay lords, four ecclesiastical lords and three other landowners of near lordly status. Peasants out for a walk must have had sore heads and arms from all the doffing of caps and tugging of forelocks involved. Since village churches so often derive from the chapels built to serve established thanes and their households, the manor house site must frequently have been the original focus of settlement in a village. In Wales various medieval estate centres are known to have stood on the sites of Roman villas. However, one cannot draw too many conclusions from the situation of the manor house or houses in a village today, for as estates prospered during the first half of the Middle Ages a lord often abandoned a house in a cramped high-street site that was bordered by smelly peasant hovels and moved to a more spacious setting on the village margins. The lord might be a permanent resident of the manor house and hardly less uncouth than the peasants he exploited or a minor knight scarcely able to support the horse and arms that his position demanded. But he might be a great lord holding a dozen or more manors and visiting each for only so long as was needed for his retinue to devour the local produce and game.

The sites of medieval manor houses are often marked by the earthworks of the rectangular moats which surrounded them. These homestead moats became exceedingly numerous, with more than 5000 of them being dug between 1150 and 1300. Lords and up-and-coming yeomen lacking the right or the income to build a castle could at least live within miniature castle moats. Whether these moats offered protection against any more serious threats than those posed by a drunken peasant was another question. Duxford in Cambridgeshire, a village which coalesced from several components, had four manor houses and the outlines of three rectangular medieval moats have been traced.

The importance of the manor house may have declined with the demise of the manor court, but churches still played important roles in the life and fabric of the village. In some cases villages must have grown up around existing churches, while in others the church was a later addition to the village. The village of Middlesmoor, overlooking Nidderdale, developed from a monastic 'grange' or abbey farm, but the origins of settlement here must go much deeper, for the elevated church site is associated with a Saxon preaching cross erected in the early days of Christian worship. It is claimed that circular and oval churchyards are legacies of pre-Saxon and monastic churches. Such churches might have been the ancient focal points of settlement at places like Sherburn in Elmet, near Leeds, where the church stands in a vast and ancient embanked enclosure, or Bramham, near Tadcaster, where the road winds around the oval churchyard.

In the wilder parts of the country, however, villages could be centuries old before they obtained a church. In the Yorkshire Dales and the Lake District there were very few medieval churches and their parishes were vast. Sometimes the villages gained late medieval chapels to reduce the difficulties – indeed dangers – of travel to church, but at other times a Victorian Methodist chapel was the first ecclesiastical building to appear. Villagers confronting blizzards and swollen rivers on their long trek to worship at a distant northern church might have envied the congregation of Swaffham Prior near Cambridge, who had two churches standing in their churchyard – the result of rivalry between two local manors.

The evidence from broken pottery shows that in many villages the earliest homes and farmsteads were clustered around the church, even if the core of the village later drifted away from this nucleus. Churches frequently mark the birthplaces of villages, even though there were some churches which always stood apart. Such foundations must have taken over sites hallowed by pagan worship or have been placed in localities where villages were slow and sporadic in forming. The church of St Michael stands alone on Brentor, a conical hill on the flanks of Dartmoor. It is ringed by the girdle of ramparts of an ancient hillfort and is said to have been founded as an act of contrition by the Norman Robert Giffard around 1150. The hilltop

Segenhoe church in Bedfordshire stands roofless some seven centuries after its surrounding village community moved to a new castle-guarded site on a distant hill.

site could well have been used for pagan worship. In 1231 Tavistock Abbey began to hold its annual fairs here.

Members of another important group of isolated churches were once surrounded by the dwellings of villages which were destined to be deserted. Among the scores of examples there is Segenhoe in Bedfordshire, still used by a congregation for more than six centuries after the villagers drifted away to a new site around a castle in approximately 1200. Then again there were villages which lost churches. Beachamwell still has a delightful Saxon church with a thatched roof and a flint round tower, but in medieval times the Norfolk village could boast three churches, each possibly associated with an ancient settlement site. Decline in the fortunes of a village was often marked by alterations to the church that had become far too large for the remaining congregation. In some cases the nave was reduced in size, in others the chancel was demolished in order to match the fallen number of worshippers. On the Suffolk coast the greatly reduced and partly ruined churches at Walberswick and Covehithe bear witness to happier days when commerce could sustain palatial buildings.

Of course, the main components of the medieval village anatomy were the dwellings themselves. In many picture-postcard villages the streets are lined with terraces of old cottages. However, terraces were not a feature of the Saxon or Norman village landscape. They developed at a much later period when roadside congestion obliged cottage dwellers to live cheek by jowl. In some medieval villages the cots and farmsteads stood individually in the paddock-sized, roughly rectangular enclosures known as closes. More commonly, particularly in planned villages, each home stood close to the roadside at one

Covehithe, Suffolk, lost much of its parish to the encroachment of the sea. Its splendid church, bereft of its congregation, was left to decay.

extremity of a long, narrow plot or 'toft' which ran back at right angles to the road. As an item of property, the toft generally remained fixed, but within it the house site could wander a few feet this way or that with each rebuilding. As we shall see, the peasant dwellings were as mean as could be, but they were freestanding within their tofts. Commonly the ends of the tofts furthest from the through road terminated at a line which could be marked by a back lane or by a bank and hedge, emphasizing the junction with the communal fields. In lots of places a zone of little privately owned or tenanted pastures filled the area between the tofts or closes and these fields.

In a single-row village, usually a small and unexciting sort of a place, there was settlement on just one side of the village through road. In two-row villages, a very common form of medieval layout, the homes would face each other across the village street. Another medieval arrangement consisted of two such rows with a short row or 'headrow' across the top to give the place a 'T'-shaped or else a triangular form. Old maps, like Elizabethan estate maps or the tithe maps of the nineteenth century, reveal how the features of the medieval village were combined in particular villages. Although tofts have often been amalgamated or subdivided, the clear outlines of medieval layouts survive in countless English villages today.

Every part of the village scene has a meaning, even though it may now be very difficult to interpret this meaning. The village is a jigsaw puzzle of components such as the green, manors, the church and house rows. Seldom can we discover who was responsible for laying the first piece on the rural board, while unlike the easier puzzles, the village could swap components and change its form through time.

5 Life in the medieval village

The medieval villager is a rather shadowy figure. Being illiterate, he or she could not record hopes, fears, convictions and beliefs. Since the villager was humble and servile, nobody else considered his or her feelings or way of life to be worthy of note. Instead, we encounter the villagers indirectly, via terse entries in the rolls of medieval manors, where they appear as the subjects of fines and as the owers of obligations. Historical documents are unable on their own to show the village peasant as a colourful, three-dimensional individual, but archaeology has recently been able to tell us a great deal about medieval village homes, while the excavation of churchyards reveals information about the ailments which afflicted the old communities.

The medieval records reveal villagers as people bowed down by work and exploited at every turn. Their only contact with learning and spiritual affairs came via a church which seems to have done its best to fill them with guilt and foreboding. Perhaps they really were wretched and down-trodden people. And perhaps this grim perception is severely flawed.

In the course of the last two or three decades archaeology has answered many questions about the medieval village home. Some of the dwellings have long since crumbled into the dust, but in other places their footings can be seen quite plainly in the turf at deserted village sites. Excavations can provide precise answers about the floor area of a house, its internal divisions and the positions of things like hearths and ovens, though it is usually less forthcoming on features which existed above ground level. The height of walls, the method of roof construction and the materials used for thatching can remain debatable. The choice of building materials varied from place to place

Gathering grapes: a scene from one of the capitals of Wells Cathedral, reminding us that there were once vineyards in England.

and from time to time, while towards the end of the Middle Ages some of the more affluent villagers were able to aspire to houses which, though barely habitable by modern standards, were much better than any occupied before. In general it is safe to characterize the village home as being small, bereft of amenities and quite likely to collapse within the lifetime of its residents and its builder.

Most peasants were farmers or smallholders as well as farm labourers, so their houses, in a sense, were farmsteads. Often the milk cows or ewes commanded as much space in the home as their owners. There was never a standard English peasant house in the Middle Ages, but the most commonly found kind was a 'long-house'. Small, long and narrow and lacking an upper storey – or indeed windows in most cases – the long-house generally consisted of two rooms divided by a short passage which ran from the door at the front to the one at the back of the house. One room was for livestock, whose body heat must have helped to warm the dwelling, and the other one was a living and sleeping room for the whole family. Sanitary arrangements were not poor, they simply did not exist, and while peat may have smouldered in a hearth at the centre of the room, much cooking was probably done outside. Chimneys were also lacking, so that smoke swirled among the rafters until it filtered through the thatch or escaped through a smoke hole at the top of the gable.

At Wharram Percy in Yorkshire almost all the village dwellings were long-houses, rectangular in shape and ranging from 49 feet (15 metres) to 75 feet (23 metres) long. Their width was often less than a third of their length. Here the excavations revealed a change in the choice of building materials, for while homes continued to be thatched, in the early part of the thirteenth century the use of timber-framing was abandoned in favour of building walls of locally quarried chalk blocks, bonded together by clay rather than mortar. Then, around 1500, the fashion for timber-framing returned, but this time the houses were built on footings of stone.

Peasant dwellings of the long-house type seem to have appeared in England around the end of the twelfth century and became very widespread in the thirteenth century. More sophisticated and solid versions remained in use until well after the close of the Middle Ages – and in remote parts of France a few were still occupied by people, sheep and cattle in the middle of the present century. However, in some medieval villages, such as Gomeldon in Wiltshire, there was a transition from the long-house to the farm house. In the twelfth century a crude long-house was built, its roof supported by curving branches joined at their tips to form a 'cruck frame', with its oven being placed in an adjoining outhouse. In the thirteenth century two larger long-houses were built close to the site of the former house, but later in the century one became a byre and the other a farm house. A farmyard was set out in front of the farm house and a large barn was built on another side of the yard. In this way there was an evolution to the 'courtyard farm', consisting of farm buildings set around a yard.

Not all medieval village homesteads were long-houses. There were two- and even three-roomed dwellings in which none of the living space was allocated to animals. At the Weald and Downland Museum at Singleton in West Sussex there is a full-scale reconstruction of a flint-walled homestead based on excavations at the deserted Sussex village of Hangleton. Here building in flint nodules replaced the use of timber around the middle of the thirteenth century. The reconstructed house has a larger and a smaller room and, with its low flint walls crowned by a great hipped roof of thatch, it provides a dramatic evocation of the medieval village scene.

During the thirteenth century rebuilding works converted scores of English villages composed of rather rickety timber shacks into villages of stone houses. These improvements certainly made the homes a little more durable, even though their walls seldom stood more than shoulder high and the roofs of poles and thatch which they bore may have been prone to collapse. One of the most rewarding deserted medieval village sites lies in the shadow of the great rocks at Hound Tor on Dartmoor, where an excavation has exposed the footings of the dwellings. Saxons had put their sunken huts here and the houses built in the early part of the twelfth century were still small and rectangular, no more than 13 feet (4 metres) in length. The walls were made firstly by erecting a wattle fence marking the inner house dimensions and secondly by building up turf blocks against the fence. Consisting of little more than twigs and soil, these dwellings had a short life and needed to be rebuilt several times. Around 1200 there was a change to building in stone, with granite rubble being gathered from the fields and moor and used to replace the insubstantial former walls.

As the Middle Ages drew towards a close, at least some members of the village community enjoyed distinct improvements to their homes. Open hearths and smoke holes were superseded by chimneys, and lofts reached by ladders sometimes became upper storeys. Windows were made and some were even glazed. In the fourteenth and fifteenth centuries lords, merchants and the most prosperous of the yeomen were able to aspire to village houses so substantial that parts of them survive to this day. For most villagers, however, the

Above: a reconstruction of a medieval house from the village of Hangleton, deserted in the fourteenth century.

Right: a reconstructed medieval house interior at the Weald and Downland Museum in West Sussex, showing the earthen floor, open hearth and minimal furniture.

living conditions remained poor. This is not to say that the peasant families enjoyed living in filth. Floors of packed earth were strewn with rushes and there is some evidence that housewives worked hard with the besom to clean their floors as best they could. Even so, the village house may have been more of a shelter than a home and much domestic life was probably enacted outside its narrow portals, away from the gloom, the stench of the byre and the choking smoke from the hearth. In the nearby manor house the lord probably owned a chair, a long table and benches for his guests and a chest as well. The poky homes of his tenants might have been completely unfurnished, apart from a sack of straw for a bed, a stool and a cot.

Most of what we know about medieval villagers has been gleaned from contemporary manorial documents which record their obligations and misdemeanours. It is not possible to describe a typical village family with any accuracy. However, we can invent a household and make its members as representative of the villagers of the thirteenth century as we can.

The scene is set in a village of the Midland counties. Robert and Alice ate Mere are resting in their garden plot, down wind of the rows of peas and beans and up wind of their pigsty. Their family name reflects the fact that one of Robert's forbears lived beside either a mere or a boundary. Surnames are still flexible and Robert's descendants may adopt ones that are different. It is Sunday and soon the tolling will summon them back to the huge stone palace which towers over the village shanties like a great ocean liner moored amongst a fleet of fishing smacks. They always like to approach the church from the east, for old traditions no less hallowed than the Christian creed warn that it is unlucky to move against the course of the sun or 'withershins'. You can only face the Devil by turning from west to east. As they walk towards the boulder-strewn swamp that is the village street their shoulders brush the thatch of their home, triggering a flurry of scuffling from the rats in the rafters. Also from within comes a gentle lowing from the family milk cow. By far their most valuable possession, it will certainly be seized by the lord on the day that Robert dies.

Although they were raised in the same village, Robert and Alice were never childhood sweethearts. Robert was already doing a man's work on his father's holding by the time that Alice was born. Robert had several flirtations – but Walter ate Mere would not countenance marriage until he felt ready to pass on his holding. Walter chose the bride. The qualities he sought in his daughter-in-law were the ability to work as hard as some men and the evidence of good breeding stock. A go-between was despatched and Henry Townsend, like any peasant with a good ewe or sow to sell, made the best deal that he could for his daughter. The dowry and the dower of land to be settled on Alice when her husband died were agreed and Henry went to survey the ate Mere holding. A hand fasting, or troth plighting, ceremony was followed by an open-air feast and thus, in the eyes of the village, Robert and Alice became man and wife. A few weeks later a more formal marriage service was performed at the door of the church.

Walter moved into a cottage hastily erected at the end of the garden and surrendered his holding at the manor court or 'hallmote.' Robert paid a stiff entry fine for the right to take over the tenancy, but the fathers were pleased that a marriage had been made within the manor. Otherwise there would have been much heavier fines to pay.

Alice is still in her mid-twenties, yet already she has given birth to five children. One died at birth and another in infancy. If the three surviving sons all reach maturity, then Robert will face a difficult choice, for only one of them, not necessarily the oldest, may inherit the holding. The two unfortunate sons may inherit money, if there is any, and may seek employment elsewhere, perhaps as mercenaries, quarrymen or tanners. With the greatest of luck one might secure a vacant holding on this or another manor, while almost unimaginable good fortune would involve marriage to a free heiress. Through such a marriage the serf himself could be made free – though the children might still be regarded as serfs. Alternatively, the sons might stay at home to help their more fortunate brother. But if they did so they

In the medieval village old pagan beliefs mixed with Christian sentiments. As late as 1471 the fertility symbol of a green man or man o' the woods was included as a footrest on the tomb of Sir Robert Whittington and his wife at Aldbury church in the Chilterns.

93

could never marry. A marriage required not only a bride but also a holding of land.

The tyranny of land over life was an all-pervading feature of the medieval village community. It remains so in some of the more sheltered Irish societies, while the old English values were exported to North America. There folk songs recalling the old habits survived in the Appalachian mountains long after they had been forgotten in the shires which gave them birth. The ballad of Lord Thomas is an example:

> Father, come father, come riddle to me,
> Come riddle it all in one,
> And tell me whether to marry Fair Ellen
> Or bring the Brown girl home?
>
> The Brown girl she has house and land,
> Fair Ellender she has none,
> And there I charge you with the blessing
> To bring the Brown girl home.

In the same way the haunting Irish ballad, 'Bunclody', tells of an age-old sadness enduring almost to this day:

> 'Tis why my love left me, you might understand
> For she has a freehold and I have no land
> She has great store of riches in silver and gold
> And everything fitting a house to uphold
>
> If I were a clerk and could write a fine hand
> I would write my love a letter and she might understand
> But I am a poor fellow who is wounded in love
> Once I lived in Bunclody but now must remove
>
> So fare thee well father, my mother adieu
> My sisters and brothers farewell unto you
> I am bound for America my fortune to try
> When I think of Bunclody I am ready to die.

Robert ate Mere is a villein. He does not like to be called such, but a villein he is. After the Norman Conquest lawyers tried to superimpose simple principles of Roman law on the complex societies of Saxon England and decided that men were either free or else serfs or villeins. Robert is certainly not free, but neither is he a slave. On the one hand, he technically owns nothing – all his goods belong to the lord of the manor, who could also sell Robert if he so wished. On the other hand, his position is protected by a great body of revered manorial custom. He is best regarded as a tenant burdened with massive obligations to provide labour and lacking any right of appeal outside or beyond the manor court.

The villeins are the powerhouse of village farming. They are more than a class and might be regarded as an estate. Often a man's identity is subsumed into this estate. If certain works are performed poorly, then a fine may be imposed on the whole of the villein workforce. At the same time the villeins as a body take many of the important decisions about farming the manor and form a jury at the manor court to sit in judgment on their fellows. Exploited, oppressed and sometimes starving, they, more than any other group, are the backbone of the realm.

Villeins behave in an obedient, even servile manner so long as they believe that the burdens imposed upon them are in accord with the ancient customs of the manor. But once they think that these hallowed traditions are being abused and flouted, they become angry and intransigent. In 1291, for example, the Abbot of Ramsey's villeins at Broughton near Huntingdon walked out of the harvest field at noon because they believed that the loaves provided for their lunchtime meal were smaller than those offered in previous years. The harvest was badly damaged and the villeins as a body were fined some 40s (about £2 today), but they had made their point.

Robert's holding consists of about thirty plough strips scattered throughout the great fields of the village. He also has a share in the brookside meadows and rights to pasture a number of beasts on the common. In return for his holding he is obliged to work on his lord's demesne on two days a week and to perform a number of 'boon works'. Notionally he does these out of the kindness of his heart, but in reality he has no choice in the matter. The only difference of substance between the boon work and the day-to-day drudgery is that on the former occasions the lord provides a lunch or dinner. Most of the servile work is similar to that which Robert performs on his own land – ploughing, sowing, harvesting, hay-making and so on – but as one of the most respected villeins, he occasionally attracts more unusual duties. In August he takes the lord's cart to the coast to buy salted herrings for the villagers who are all engaged in boon works in the harvest fields. This task takes him away from the village for five days – at a time when he feels desperate to secure his own harvest. Nevertheless, it gives him a wonderful opportunity to catch up with the affairs of the nation, to converse with peasants speaking in the strange accents of other counties and to glimpse the fantastic building works being undertaken at church, cathedral and castle sites along the way. Every scene and snippet of gossip is absorbed into his memory, for he knows that on his return he will face relentless

Medieval lords were generally hard and masterful – as expressed in the tomb effigy of one of the Marmion dynasty at West Tanfield, near Ripon.

quizzing from the other villagers when they take their harvest dinner in the lord's house.

At Christmas Robert gives his lord a hen. This is a payment made for the right to gather firewood in the lord's wood. Robert is careful to select the bird which lays the fewest eggs and looks most ready to meet its maker. He also makes a gift of ale – but then the villagers go to the hall and have a Christmas dinner comprising most of what they have just given. Robert is also the subject of more serious obligations. When he dies, his best beast will be taken as a heriot by the lord and the second best will be commandeered by the church – the same church that regularly takes a tithe (one tenth) of every item of value which the family produces. These fines or taxes, along with those for 'entering' or inheriting his holding, make it very hard for the family to prosper from the fruits of their toil.

It is less easy to itemize all the work that Alice performs; Robert is the head of the household and they are his duties and failings which are listed in the manor rolls. However, the medieval village is not such a male-dominated world as one might imagine. Women can hold and sublet land and careful provisions are made for widows, some of whom work holdings with their own or hired labour after the death of their husbands. Alice is more than a mother and a housewife. She looks after the family poultry and she also attends to urgent jobs on the holding on the many days when Robert is conscripted for work on the lord's demesne. Then, along with all the able-bodied adults and children, she becomes part of the throng engaged in boon works at harvest and haytime.

Villeins are not the only community within the village. The free tenants also form a coherent group, one which is no less forthright in its determination to preserve its ancient rights and status. Because freedom can be enjoyed in a variety of different and complicated ways – some are generally regarded as being free, while others tenant land which has a free status attached to it – disputes are frequent. They certainly cannot be resolved by reference to factors like material wealth, for it is perfectly possible to be both free and yet poorer than any family of villeins on the manor. On the whole, villagers are free if the other free families in the village accept them into their ranks. It is also generally the case that the obligations of work service associated with free tenure soon become replaced by money rents. This makes it easier for the ambitious free family to rise in the world, for any money remaining after the payment of rents and tithes can be invested to expand the holding. Though free of obligations to provide manual labour, the freemen or franklins often ride on errands for the lord and can serve as supervisors at times when the village labour force is assembled together at harvest. The medieval village is packed with thrusting individualists determined to better their lot.

When the villein feels the need to look down upon someone, as doubtless he sometimes does, he can always cast a superior glance at the cottars. The structure of village society is complicated, but in descending order the classes are composed of freemen or franklins; husbonds or geneats or villeins; and cottars. The cottars have much smaller holdings than the villeins; their name refers to the fact that they live in the smallest of the village dwellings – the cots or cottages – rather than in the houses occupied by the husbonds, who are bondsmen with houses. Cottars are defined by the small size of their holdings rather than their class status. Some cottars are also free men. Having little land to work, the cottars have only a modest burden of services and survive by supplementing the produce of their holdings with wages earned by working for others. The lowest of the cottars are not tenants of the lord but subtenants of one of their village neighbours, while even those cottars who do work on the demesne toil not alongside the villeins but as a separate body. Certain cottars serve as the lord's ploughman, shepherd and cowherd but they can never aspire to the high estate offices, which are always manned by villeins.

Not everybody in the village fits easily into one of these three classes. In Robert's village there are three 'anilepimen', landless farm labourers. Being landless, they are also single. One is the son of a villager who failed to receive an inheritance of land and the others drifted into the village in search of work. They are employed by some of the larger tenants. There is also a small but growing class of 'molmen', villeins who no longer serve in the field beside their fellow villeins, for they have reached an agreement with their lord and now pay cash rents for their holdings rather than performing work.

And then there are the specialists. The miller is called John Miller, a name which is not chosen by coincidence. Surnames are still rather fluid and most villagers are named after the place where they live, like Atwood or Townsend, after their trade, like Smith or Turner, or after their father, like Jackson (son of Jack). The miller is one of the most prosperous franklins and pays a very heavy rent for the tenancy of the lord's watermill, which he must also maintain and repair. His income comes from the 'multure', a share of flour which he retains from his peasant clients as a charge for milling their grain. All the villagers believe that John Miller takes an unjustly large multure. Nobody in the village speaks well of the miller, yet there is not a father who would not be delighted to see his daughter marry him.

The blacksmith is a villein and a smallholder, the plot of land which he works always being the one allocated to the smith, so that whoever tenants it is either the village blacksmith or else responsible for appointing one. The standing of the smith in village society is rather peculiar, though there are few people left who still believe that smiths are workers of magic. He ploughs like a villein but also dines in the manor like one of the lord's household servants. In fact, he serves both communities, providing shares and coulters for the village ploughs and shoeing both the plough horses and the mounts of the lord. He bridges the gap between the communities of the village and the manor. The household of the manor includes servants or 'famuli' as well as agricultural workers, such as a ploughman, shepherd, swineherd and cowman who work on the manor farm. These agricultural workers are cottars who toil at their specialist occupations and have no other duties.

Then there is a small class of officials. The most important of these is the reeve, who serves the lord and village as a sort of general foreman. He is invariably a villein of the more substantial and reliable kind and was elected by the village community whose members knew that they would all be fined should their choice prove a bad one. As he fills a most demanding office, the reeve is excused all other duties, invited to dine at the lord's table during harvest and allowed to pasture his horse on the demesne. He is responsible for the conduct of the farm work on the manor and also acts as a rent collector for the lord, witnesses wills and even has the power to sanction or prevent marriages by daughters who hope to wed outside the village.

Villagers of a lower standing serve the lord as woodward, hayward and beadle. The woodward guards the woods of the manor, making sure that the villagers take no more than their entitlement to fallen twigs for fuel and timber for repairing hedges and ploughs. The hayward is responsible for keeping horn and corn well apart and for ensuring that visitors from neighbouring parishes do not steal shocks of ripened grain around harvest time. The beadle helps the reeve to organize village husbandry and collect rents; he also serves as the officer of the manor court and collects fines. Doubtless his vocation makes him unpopular with his neighbours and his humble status makes him an even more likely target for derision than the miller.

There is another minor official who is also associated with fines levied by the lord of the manor, but his job is much more coveted than that of the beadle. This is the aletaster, who samples all the brews fermented in the peasant households and offered for sale to ensure that they reach the standards set by the royal assize of ale. As there are many brewers and fines are frequently imposed, we can be sure that the aletasters perform their duties with a rare gusto.

Last, but certainly not least, there is the priest. Were the parish a notably rich one, then it would probably be served by a priest from an aristocratic background. Were it a poor one, then the priest will probably be an illiterate fellow who had risen from the ranks of the peasants. In this case, the parish suffers from having an absentee rector whose place is filled by Henry, a vicar who was born a villein and whose proud father paid the lord a hefty fine to allow the boy to take holy orders. Henry learned what he could about the services and ritual by serving as a chaplain and now he struggles with an office which is really more than he can master, stumbling through the Latin mass that the congregation do not understand. He lives in constant fear that a visitation by the bishop will expose his lack of learning. Henry is paid a wage by the affluent rector who claims the harvest of parish tithes, but it is not a living wage. He is both a vicar and a peasant farmer and relies heavily on the food he can raise by farming the glebe land. His life involves a repetitive sequence of changes from being the tonsured and cowled representative of a mystical and unfathomable religion to toiling in the rain and cold to scratch a living from the land. When the babies of the village are christened, they are held in rough hands soiled by the same earth which gave them birth.

The village is riddled with class distinctions and it is never easy to breach the barriers of status. The whole fabric of society and survival depends upon people knowing their place in it and meeting their obligations. It would be easy to imagine that the village is a world of separate cells and has no all-embracing identity. But this does not seem to be the case. People talk about 'the blood of the village' and are always reluctant to see an outsider take up a vacant holding if there is a true-born villager available as a potential tenant. The manor court rolls also reveal what appears to be a paranoid fear of outsiders, for villagers are frequently being fined for harbouring strangers. Faced with a heavy burden of harvest work, a villein is easily tempted to hire and lodge one or two farm workers who are 'foreigners' from outside the village. Perhaps the harsh reaction of the manor court reflects fears that the feudal structures could collapse if men became free to come and go as they pleased. The village as a whole is always particularly anxious to prevent any of its members from bringing in stock belonging to outsiders, for the grazing resources of the common are limited and cannot be shared with foreign beasts.

The harsh realities of life were interspersed by various festivities in the village year. There is little evidence of the existence of communal village buildings at this time, although an intriguing snippet of information was recorded by Walter Map, an official in the court of Henry II, in his *Courtiers' Trifles*. Writing in 1182 of a time about a century earlier, he told how Edric Wild was returning from the hunt when he found a large building on the edge of the forest. Light streamed from the windows, but when he peered inside he saw noble ladies dancing – and all were phantoms. He said that this was a building 'such as the English have as drinking-houses, one in each parish called in English "ghildhus" '.

Bench ends at Altarnun church, Cornwall, give a lively picture of the more festive side of life in the later Middle Ages. The armed figure (upper right) is probably a sword-dancer rather than a warrior.

Not a great deal is known about the games and festivals of the thirteenth century, although by the end of the Middle Ages forms of Morris dancing and various boisterous, even dangerous, ball games existed. Some of the festivities enjoyed in the village must have been inherited from pagan times, particularly those associated with May time. On the eve of May Day, the young people of the village often

seem to have passed the night in the nearby fields, engaging in dalliance or rather more. Shortly afterwards there were the 'gangdays', when the bounds of the parish were beaten. The small boys of the village followed the cross and banners were buffeted against the boundary landmarks, the better to remember the extent of the communal territory. To underline the pagan nature of the rituals, at certain points which might be marked by 'holy' trees the procession would halt and the priest would extend a blessing over the emerging crops. Then there was the next great feast of the religious year, Whitsuntide (the other ones being Christmas and Easter). The Christian successor to the pagan midsummer ceremonies took place on the eve of the Nativity of St John the Baptist, 24 June. Bonfires were lit, flaming brands were carried around the fields and at night in some places flaming wheels were sent rolling down the hillsides. The origins of these customs must have been long forgotten, but it was believed that the fires would drive away dragons, while the courses of the wheels symbolized the motions of the sun.

Then there were other celebrations which were peculiar to a certain parish or to a stage in the farming year. A wake was held on the eve of the day of the patron saint of the village church, when the members of the community, who were usually drowsy by dusk, were allowed to stay up late. On the following day, villagers who worshipped at daughter churches would process with their banners flying to the mother church – and this provided ample opportunities to engage in brawls with members of the 'home team'. When the village concerned was so favoured, the saint's day was normally also the day of the village fair. This was not only a time for commerce and games but also a day when visitors from neighbouring settlements were entertained and when departed members of the community would seek to return.

Harvest marked the end of the farming year. The cutting of the last sheaf and the leading home of the last load were celebrated by customs and rituals which varied from manor to manor, though the harvest feast, with its music and dancing, must have been universally enjoyed. All these milestones introduced an element of excitement into the perpetual cycle of reaping and sowing, ploughing and haytime. Even by the standards of the small village shows of today, the diversions on offer were rustic and humdrum, but for the peasants of the Middle Ages they answered that essential human need for something novel that would break the routine of day-to-day life.

The tedium of life could be broken in harsher ways, by sickness and by death. Some impressions of the realities of life in the medieval village have come from that least glamorous branch of archaeological endeavour, the excavation of old cess pits. The work shows that the villagers were infested by a range of intestinal parasites. Digs in medieval graveyards reveal that toothache was a common and potentially fatal ailment and was probably such a widespread curse in the village because flour was contaminated by particles of grit which ground away the enamel of teeth. Another common affliction was osteoarthritis, the price of hard toil in wet and windswept fields. The village itself might have been designed to spread epidemics; there were no sewers and no piped water supplies. For the peasants there were no doctors, nothing but the care and concern of relatives and neighbours, so that a broken leg could result in death or a lifetime of infirmity. Drinking water was obtained from wells or springs, both sources being polluted by seepages from cess pits and middens. To survive, the medieval villagers must have had a far greater resistance to disease than most of us today. But when this resistance was undermined by famine, that other lurking curse of medieval life, then numerous villagers died.

Ailments like the toothache, easily remedied today, were in the Middle Ages a source of misery and even death. This figure is from another capital in Wells Cathedral.

6 The times of dying

The life of the village was the life of its people. The life of these people was sustained by the village lands, for without haytime and harvest there could be no life. Death was always a part of life in village England, but, from the time of King Alfred until the fourteenth century, the growth in the population of villages was hardly checked at all. In the Saxon centuries villages appeared and multiplied, and this era of creation and vitality continued through Norman and Plantagenet times. These new villages were not like the ancient villages, which were born and died within the passage of a few generations. They were places which would endure and persist unless particular misfortunes befell them. Had this period of multiplication continued, then the surface of England would have become covered in settlements, each one lacking the precious resources of land needed to support a population. In the event, the environment did launch a blind retaliation against the excesses of village growth, though the human failings of greed and violence played no less important roles in the culling of flocks.

Many people believe that lost village sites are rare and remarkable places. The small minority of cases which have been thoroughly explored by archaeologists have certainly yielded invaluable information, but really lost villages are a commonplace of the country-side. Few English readers of this book will be living more than five miles from the site of one such lost village or hamlet.

Even in times when the generosity of harvests pushed thoughts of famine from the minds of countryfolk, war was always a threat to the stability of village life. The details are not recorded, but in the Dark Ages when armies or war bands passed across the countryside,

Fountains Abbey was responsible for destroying a clutch of villages; a few intruded on the solitude of the monks, but the others were on sites earmarked for monastic farms.

villages and crops must have been burned quite frequently. Yet it would normally take much more than a serious fire to extinguish the life of a settlement. When word of the approaching host arrived, villagers would scurry to drive their stock into the havens of tangled woods or uncharted marshes. Later, they would emerge to assess the destruction and then begin to build anew in the place where the ashes of their lost abodes were still warm.

A far more systematic programme of destruction was undertaken by William the Conqueror in his Harrying of the North of 1069–71. This 'scorched earth' policy was not inflicted upon a hostile army so much as upon those of his subjects who were unfortunate enough to live in the rebellious north. Orderic Vitalis, who was born in 1075, when the memory of the slaughter was still fresh, described the Harrying as William's most cruel act and he recounted how crops, herds and food of every kind were gathered together and burned. He believed that 100,000 men, women and children, all Christians of the north, had perished in the famine that followed.

Another chronicler, Symeon of Durham, wrote that: 'Between York and Durham no village was inhabited'. He described a northern land which lay desolate for nine years, and certainly when Domesday Book was compiled in 1086 almost 45 per cent of the manors in Yorkshire were still wholly or partly wasted. But the countryside did not remain desolate for ever more. Swarms of new villages were created to repopulate the wasted estates and many were built to planned layouts with precisely measured dimensions. During the centuries that followed there may have been other villages which were exterminated in the course of warfare, but examples are not easily found. Leake, on the margins of the North York Moors, might be an example. There is a robust Norman church close to the busy A19 routeway and little else, but in 1852 a pit full of skeletons was discovered here. Along with the townlet of Northallerton, Leake was burned in 1318, when Sir James Douglas brought a host of 5000 raiders down from Scotland – and local tradition claims that the village was never again inhabited.

Ironically, we know more about English villages which were destroyed by men of God than by men of war. The destroyers were monks of the Cistercian order. This austere reforming order was founded towards the end of the eleventh century by St Stephen Harding, abbot of Citeaux, an Englishman, and St Bernard, abbot of Clairvaux. Bernard had a mystical devotion to the Virgin Mary and he sought to impose this devotion upon the communities of the new order. They were to live in secretive and lonely places, even in hostile and dangerous locations, for such settings would provide a foretaste of the death to come. The first Cistercian house was established in woodland at Waverley in Surrey in 1128, but soon the monks realized that a more effective divorce from the evils of the lay world could be enjoyed amidst the solitude of hidden northern places. Fountains Abbey was founded by converted Benedictines who left the abbey of St Mary at York in 1132 and adopted a harsh pioneering life at the site where their new Cistercian abbey would rise. Uninviting as this setting then was, it was not entirely deserted and the solitude which the monks desired was only achieved by the enforced eviction of village communities who unwittingly intruded upon the privacy of their new neighbours. The monks gained control of nearby Herleshow in 1149 and the next time that its name was recorded the place existed not as a village but as a monastic farm. Cayton, lying just three miles from the abbey, had met a similar fate a few years earlier. The monks seldom seem to have allowed their Christian consciences to persuade them to rehouse evicted villagers, although, as we have seen in the cases of Old Byland and East Witton, they could act with charity.

The apparent callousness of the Cistercians towards village communities must have derived partly from their obsession with solitude and partly from the way in which they managed their estates. The hallmark of Cistercian farming was the independent monastic farm or 'grange'. These monks did not rely upon the sweat and toil of servile tenants. Instead they created their own workforce of lay brothers or 'conversi'. Occupying a niche somewhere between those of the peasant and the monk, the lay brothers were housed in substantial numbers at the abbey estate headquarters and they provided the workforces at the outlying granges. While some villages perished owing to their unfortunate proximity to a chosen abbey site, many more were torn down on the expanding abbey estates as grange farming supplanted peasant tillage. Fountains Abbey alone is known to have been responsible for the destruction of six villages and is suspected of having accounted for a further sixteen villages and hamlets, while in Leicestershire at least ten villages were obliterated by other monastic clearances.

While granges destroyed villages, they also led to their creation. All the villages in Upper Nidderdale developed after the Dissolution from nuclei provided by former monastic granges; Kilnsey in Wharfedale, which nestles beside the spectacular cliff of Kilnsey crag is another and a better-known example.

The monastic village clearances, which took place as the abbey estates expanded during the twelfth and thirteenth centuries, did

little to stem the vigour of village England as a whole. Just as bands of brethren were setting forth from the older establishments to found new houses, so villagers must have been leaving overcrowded settlements to create new villages and hamlets. In the cases of a few well-documented examples we can learn how local lords sometimes masterminded the process of village and market foundation, but in general the picture is blurred. What we do know is that as the choicest lands and sites became fully exploited, so colonization was steered towards the margins, with communities being established on the more windswept, dry, sandy, stony, clayey and waterlogged settings. Nature's chessboard was becoming crowded with pieces, but this chessboard was not constant and could change its nature. Places which provided meagre sustenance when the climate was friendly could offer only starvation when temperatures shifted by just a degree or two. On the margins of village England a late spring, a little more cloud than expected in July or autumnal rain storms at harvest could spell disaster.

Between the Saxon period and the fourteenth century the growth of villages had been nurtured by a steadily improving climate which had lured settlers into places that would otherwise have seemed uninviting. Thirteenth-century England had rung to the tune of the axe as lands uncultivated since Roman times were cleared to sustain the swelling population of peasants. But in the fourteenth century the climatic downturn became obvious. Summers were cool and wet and the winters stormy. In the clay vales the ground could not absorb the mounting rainfall. Fields where grain had grown stayed cold and wet in the spring – and so they were converted to pasture.

Meanwhile, settlers were retreating from the sodden, cloud-hung uplands. In many barren places the people of the small villages and hamlets tried to compensate for falling yields by increasing the intensity of their efforts. But their actions only accelerated the exhaustion of the soil and hastened the day of desertion.

For many young villages situated in the vulnerable margins of the agricultural arena, death involved a gradual decay and desertion, and, when the communities disappeared, no written epitaph or record was left. Their only memorial was composed of the troughs in the ground which had been roads and ditches and the level platforms where houses had once stood.

There were other places where death was violent and dramatic. These were the coastal villages which were undermined or swept away in the great sea storms unleashed by a climate in torment. Since Roman times more than eighty square miles of land have been washed from the coast of Holderness. Villages and towns known to have perished there include Wilsthorpe, Auburn, Hartburn, Hyde, Withow, Cleton, Northorpe, Hornsea Burton, Hornsea Beck, South-orpe, Great Colden, Colden Parva, Old Aldbrough, Ringborough, Monkwell, Monkwike, Sand-le-Mere, Waxholme, Owthorne, New-sham, Old Withernsea, Out Newton, Dimlington, Tumarr, Northorp, Hoton, Old Kilnsea, Ravenspurn and the medieval trading port of Ravenser-Odd. Then, on the Humber side of Spurn Head, Tharles-thorpe, Frismersk, Penisthorpe, East Somerte, Orwithfleet, Sunthorpe and Burstall Priory have been lost. Not all these places perished in the storms of the fourteenth century. The climate continued to deteriorate until it reached the depths of the 'little ice age' of 1600–1750. Today new sea defences are urgently being built to preserve what remains of the village of Mappleton, which overlooks the watery graves of its former east-coast neighbours. Of course, if the starker predictions about global warming or the 'greenhouse effect' are realized, then the former events on the Holderness coast will seem trivial in comparison.

Only now are we beginning to appreciate – and perhaps not in time – that the environment which sustains us can prove vindictive when abused. This fact certainly applied to the relatively recent demise of the Devon fishing village of Hallsands. Towards the end of the nineteenth century shingle was dredged from Start Bay and used in the construction of the dockyard at Devonport. Nobody paused to consider the effects that this dredging might have upon local tides and currents, and in the January of 1917 the sea swept across the little village which sat on a rock shelf at the foot of the cliffs. The people of Hallsands only escaped death by fleeing their houses and scrambling up the cliffs. Though homeless and destitute, they received no official compensation for the ill-conceived works which had ruined their lives.

In medieval times periodic local or national famines resulting from crop failures weakened peasant populations and thus exposed them to the ravages of disease. Starvation and plague together took their toll across the countryside. In the middle of the fourteenth century rural England accommodated more people than it could sustain. It was not a land of great towns and diverse opportunities, but a farming country of villages and hamlets, of which the regional capitals and market towns formed only a small part. Labour was cheap and overabundant, the margins of farming were contracting, the prevailing mood was one of anxiety and gloom and the stage was set for calamity.

Calamity arrived in the hideous form of the Black Death or the Pestilence. In 1346, the Pestilence, which was spread by rat fleas, erupted amongst a Tartar army laying siege to the Crimean city of Kaffa. It spread remorselessly across Europe and made its debut in England at Weymouth or Southampton in 1348; by the early spring of the following year London was in the grip of a terrible epidemic and the fate of the rest of Britain was decided. The country was utterly unable to resist the onslaught of a plague. The villages might have been designed for rats. The low roofs of thatch were havens for breeding, runs could weave in and out of dwellings which had shallow wall footings and earthen floors, and when an infected rat perished in the thatch above, the departing fleas could drop to new hosts slumbering in their filthy rags on straw mattresses below.

It is easy to see that the villages of the English grainlands were rat-infested places in which the Pestilence could wreak the most awful havoc. Nevertheless, the disease appears to have been no less lethal amongst monastic communities, where much higher standards of hygiene prevailed, and in the northern areas of livestock farming, where villages and grain stores were fewer and smaller. The disease continued to erupt periodically throughout the Middle Ages and remained a lurking threat during the seventeenth century.

Some experts have estimated that the Pestilence of the fourteenth century exterminated one third of the English population, others that half the population was annihilated. Wherever there is local knowledge of a lost village site, the Pestilence is invariably offered up as an explanation. Yet it is remarkably hard to trace villages that were killed by the Black Death. There are copious examples of little communities appealing to the authorities for tax relief on account of

the savagery of the plague in their locality, but very few cases which prove the power of disease alone to depopulate a village for all time. Though we should not underestimate the physical and psychological horrors of events which could, in a matter of days, leave a surviving villager bereft of most of his relatives, half of his friends and workmates and no longer able to farm the surrounding lands in a satisfactory way.

On the estate at Steeple Barton in Oxfordshire some 32 of the 36 tenants on the manor died in the initial onslaught of the Pestilence from 1349 to 1350 and more than 600 acres of land lay neglected; within four years the acreage of abandoned land had doubled and the manor house had become worthless. Oxfordshire has yielded more than its share of examples of villages directly exterminated by the Pestilence. They include Tusmore, Combe and also Tilgarsley, which had no fewer than 52 tenants before the plague, but which was said by a tax collector in 1359 to have been deserted for the last nine years.

More typically, however, the hard-hit village would endure a period during which a skeleton population struggled to survive before communal life revived completely. Woodeaton in Oxfordshire probably came as close to extinction as possible without dying. The Pestilence reduced the workforce to just two tenants who wanted to leave the stricken village. They were persuaded to remain by the abbot who controlled the estate. The village revived and shows no scars of its near demise. Cublington in Buckinghamshire was completely abandoned. Yet the name of the settlement was preserved by colonists, perhaps former villagers, who returned and built their homes on higher ground overlooking the relics of the former streets, dwellings, castle mound and fishpond.

However, if the direct consequences of the Black Death upon village England were measured in mere dozens of losses, the indirect effects caused hundreds, indeed thousands, of desertions. On the one hand, this was due to the weakening of many village communities, particularly those that had struggled to exist on poor or worn-out lands before the Pestilence. On the other hand, the survivors of the tragedies found their circumstances transformed. Before the plague there had been no vacancies in the countryside of England, but now the lords of depleted manors were all offering vacant tenancies, even seeking to woo away the tenants of their neighbours. Few lords or manorial officials would return a runaway peasant to his master and few felt so secure that they could uphold the harsh old strictures when the villeins demanded better terms.

Gradually, the servile villagers learned to flex their muscles and they sought to discover the limits of their power in the new, half-empty rural world which the Pestilence had created. The lords, meanwhile, did not find it easy to substitute hired toilers for their feudal tenants. The same grim forces that had increased the value of the tenants had also fuelled a rise in wages as the artisans and hirelings discovered the scarcity value of their labour. Meanwhile, the village villeins and cottars were realizing that the obligations of service on the lord's demesne, so loathed and resented for centuries, might finally be shattered.

On manor after manor a power struggle ensued. In the field by day and in the village at dusk, the bondsmen grumbled and plotted. In one locality after another a consensus emerged that if the lord would not substitute rent-paying tenancies for feudal service, then trouble would follow. This struggle took the form of bloody-minded work-to-rule campaigns, carefully timed strikes, sabotage or simple obstinacy. If all these tactics failed, then the disgruntled villager could simply run away in the fairly secure knowledge that work and a more indulgent master could easily be found. In this way it was recorded at Theydon Garnon in Essex in 1390 that 'Simon Jakeboy withdrew John Pretylwell from the service of Thomas Mason into his own service in the occupation of malt monger, giving him 26s. 8d. [£1.33p] and food and clothing every year.' John, it was recorded, had formerly been a servile ploughman.

Some lords accepted the apparent inevitability of the circumstances, so that countrysides formerly peopled by bondsmen were now home to a vast class of rent-paying tenants. Others also recognized the decay of demesne farming and leased their lands out to one large farmer, usually a yeoman rising in society.

Amongst the ranks of both the lords and the yeomen there were hard-faced individuals who realized that land could yield a tidy income by employing a mere handful of workers, namely shepherds. These individuals had no thoughts of attracting labour but of evicting it. The most likely targets for eviction were the weaker villages which were emaciated by the decay of their environment and by the onslaughts of the Black Death. For centuries, England's wealth had been based on the export of wool. The Cistercians had long since demonstrated just how productive effectively run sheep ranges could be. Until Tudor times peasant tillage had been but little disrupted by competition with sheep, while under the old feudal system each lord had at least a nominal obligation to protect his tenants and their land resources. Then the old stability of village society was shaken away by the Peasants' Revolt of 1381, when insurgents from Kent and Essex took the Tower of London. On manor after manor the records of servitude were destroyed and the clerks who could rewrite the details were attacked. The Revolt was partly an attack on the continuation of villeinage, fuelled by the egalitarian attitudes to Christianity associated with John Wyclif and John Ball. It was partly a response to the toll taken by the interminable wars in France. But most directly it was a revolt against the unjust poll tax of 1380. It was against this background of trauma and jarring change that the greatest ever assault on village England took place.

At the start of the fourteenth century England was exporting about 30,000 sacks of wool each year, but the trade in wool declined as native spinners and weavers were encouraged to convert the harvest into cloth. By the end of the century the exports of raw wool had been halved, although cloth exports had greatly increased. By 1485 England was exporting 50,000 cloths, each cloth being 72 feet long and just over 5 feet broad. It was in this same year that State Inquiries began to collect and record information, which tells us about the wholesale destruction of villages, a process which had already gathered some momentum. It would continue until the early sixteenth century in the Midlands and through the Elizabethan era in the north. The motive for the destruction was profit. As one sixteenth-century pamphleteer wrote: '. . . who will maintain husbandry which is the nurse of every County as long as sheep bring so great

Substantial, ivy-encrusted and flower-garlanded village houses, like these at Long Melford, in Suffolk, give a completely false impression of the medieval village house.

gain? who will be at cost to keep a dozen in his house to milk kine [cattle], make cheese, carry it to the market when one poor soul may by keeping sheep get him a greater profit . . . who will not be contented for to pull down houses of husbandry so that he may stuff his bags full of money?'

John Rous, a chantry priest of Warwick who died in 1491, left a clear statement of his revulsion towards events that he had witnessed: 'What shall be said of the modern destruction of villages which brings Death to the commonwealth? The root of this evil is greed. The plague of avarice infects these times and it blinds men. They are not sons of God, but of Mammon.'

The sons of Mammon who evicted villagers, tore down their dwellings, converted the village ploughlands into sheep pastures and enclosed the estate with hedgerows came from several backgrounds, but most were local men. Some, like the notorious Knightleys of Fawsley in Northamptonshire, belonged to the land-owning nobility and some, like the Spencers of Wormleighton in Warwickshire, had risen from yeoman backgrounds. It was mainly in the sixteenth century, when the worst of the evictions were past, that speculators from outside, like wool merchants, clothiers, tanners, lawyers and goldsmiths became involved in buying and depopulating land. The evictors were sometimes the very people responsible for upholding justice. In 1478 an estate at Steeton in Yorkshire was purchased by Chief Justice Fairfax. Shortly afterwards the small village community of around thirty adults was evicted and the site of the settlement incorporated into a manor park. In 1525 the last traces of the dwellings were obliterated by the creation of a great ornamental pond.

The scale of the destruction throughout the Midlands, parts of East Anglia and eastern Yorkshire was amazing. At a time when four or five decades of assaults on village England still had to take place, John Rous was able to list some fifty-eight villages which he knew had been destroyed. Professor M. W. Beresford was able to identify all bar one of these places, and all lay within just a dozen miles of Warwick. But the scale of destruction in Warwickshire could also be encountered in Northamptonshire, Leicestershire, Oxfordshire and several other counties. The theme of the once bustling countryside that was now occupied only by the shepherd and his dog occurs again and again in the writings of the fifteenth and early sixteenth centuries. The most famous expression of it was provided by Sir Thomas More in *Utopia*.

The sheep that were wont to be so meek and tame and so small eaters now, as I hear say, be become so great devourers and so wild that they eat up and

swallow down the very men themselves. They consume, destroy and
devour whole fields, houses and cities.
One shepherd or herdsman is enough to eat up that ground with cattle to
the occupying whereof about husbandry many hands were requisite.
Look in what parts of the realm doth grow the finest and therefore dearest
wool, there noblemen and gentlemen: yea and certain Abbots . . . leave no
ground for tillage, they enclose all into pasture: they throw down houses:
they pluck down towns [i.e. villages] and leave nothing standing but only
the church to be made a sheep-cote.

The dissent surrounding the destruction of villages in Tudor times
had more than just a moral dimension. In 1488 a special act was
passed to stem the depopulation of the Isle of Wight, where the
destruction of more than twenty villages raised the threat of French
occupation. More universal was the fear of serious revolt as the lanes
of England filled with bitter, dispossessed villagers. In 1489
legislation was enacted against the 'Pulling Down of Towns'. A
series of acts in the sixteenth century attempted to reverse the
clearances, but successful prosecutions were few and far between.
Some desertions were blamed by the accused upon the Black Death,
while those under investigation could often argue, quite truthfully,
that the evictions had taken place before the introduction of
legislation. But it was very much the case that the investigating
commissioners found it distasteful to side with grumbling and
inarticulate peasants against landowners of their own class and
background. Later in the sixteenth century a rise in the price of bread
grain stimulated tillage and it was this economic reality rather than
any triumph of justice which caused the sheep clearances to peter out.

In the eighteenth and nineteenth centuries the Scottish Highlands
experienced a brutal episode of clearances, suggesting that Mammon
was still at the helm of national life. In the 1890s a butcher of
Ramsbury, named Henry Wilson, bought two large farms in the
Wiltshire village of Snap. The land was converted into a sheep run
for use in Wilson's sheep-dealing ventures, and this loss of
employment in farming caused the village to be deserted amidst
scenes of controversy in which Wilson's sons successfully sued the
local MP for describing the family as oppressive and tyrannical.

By Elizabethan times the ghastly sheep clearances were virtually
over, but the pruning of the village population continued at a less
frantic level. Tillage could now compete with sheep farming, though
the decay of medieval feudalism had both bad and good consequences
for the villagers. Landowners now gained their income from rents
and leases rather than from the working of the demesne by unpaid
vassals. Where land was expected to support a large population of

Village shows and fêtes are often directly descended from medieval chartered fairs. All the simple pleasures of the old festivals are recalled at the popular end-of-summer feast at Pateley Bridge, Yorkshire (right and below).

Most medieval windmills were small and relatively flimsy, and none has survived. Those that we see today were almost all built in the eighteenth or nineteenth centuries. This one is at Denver, Norfolk.

peasants at, or a little above, the level of starvation, there was little left that could be converted into profit in the form of rents. If, however, the lord could replace a swarm of village peasants and their dependants with just a few prosperous tenants who employed their own wage-earning labourers, then higher rents could be obtained. Villagers were not evicted immediately, though in many places no opportunity was lost to buy out small freeholders or persuade copyholders to become leaseholders. In ways such as these lands worked by two dozen families could become divided between just a few large farms. The village meanwhile would shrink and crumble until all that was left were three or four farmsteads separated by empty land and a decaying church standing guard over the platforms and troughs which were once house sites and streets. It is a theme that is repeated again and again in counties such as Norfolk.

The Age of Enlightenment did not always foster more humane attitudes towards humble villagers. Between Elizabethan and Victorian times any village community living close to their lord had good reason to fear eviction – and the more wealthy and powerful the lord, the greater the threat that he posed. This new threat to villages resulted from changes in the social order and in the way that status was flaunted.

Members of the feudal aristocracy had lived rather rough and ready lives. Much time was spent in journeying between the various manors that they owned – only the most influential had castles – and social status derived from the ownership of large amounts of land, pedigree and military might. The Tudor monarchy achieved a monopoly of power in the realm, castles became redundant, while entrepreneurs and courtiers gained access to the ranks of the aristocracy. New ways of living and of proclaiming status were needed and a fashion for immensely costly mansions set in tastefully manicured grounds was born.

None of this need have posed a threat to villages, were it not for the fact that many of the old family seats earmarked for improvement had villages in very close proximity, while the creation or enlargement of parks extended private land into what had been communal territory. The relationship between the lord and his tenants had scarcely been a close one in feudal times, but the manor house had served as the administrative hub of the estate and there had been much coming and going as villagers organized their work, played their various roles in the proceedings of the manor court or arrived to enjoy one of the seasonal feasts. Now the relationship became much more remote. The lord lived with his household of family, numerous guests and domestic servants. There was little place in this tasteful setting for the grubby ploughman or foul-mouthed smith.

Those who regularly visit stately homes are likely to have noticed a similarity in many settings. Not far from the house there is often an isolated medieval church – more likely than not crammed with family memorabilia and used as a private chapel. Around the church the great lawn of the park may be humped and grooved by earthworks, while the grassland beyond is corrugated with the sinuous, curving ridges and furrows of medieval ploughland. This is the landscape of emparking. In some places a replacement village for the one or ones swept away stands deferentially outside the gates of the park, but in others the villagers were rendered utterly homeless.

One of the earliest examples of the rehousing of the evicted community took place at Holdenby in Northamptonshire around 1587. Some years earlier, Sir Christopher Hatton, destined to become Lord Chancellor to Queen Elizabeth I, had a great mansion with a classical façade built around four great courtyards. Later the garden was enlarged so that it engulfed the church and the village which stood close by. Another village stood to the north-east of the new mansion and it was rebuilt and enlarged to accommodate the displaced families. (The mansion endured for less than a century, but a smaller one was built there in the 1870s.)

Frequently the victims of emparking were the villages whose growth had been stunted or whose communities had been weakened by previous disasters. In the case of Milton in Dorset, however, the victim was not a village but a small town. Milton had existed as a market centre for at least seven centuries and had expanded in the precinct of its medieval abbey; in 1770 it supported more than one hundred households. Trouble appeared in the form of Lord Milton, formerly Joseph Damer MP. He had his house, Milton Abbey, and its grounds remodelled by William Chambers and Lancelot 'Capability' Brown, but then claimed that the presence, just beyond his garden wall, of the little town was intruding upon his privacy. Between 1771 and 1785 he systematically destroyed Milton by demolishing its homes as their leases expired. Brown and Chambers developed the nearby dry valley site for the replacement village of Milton Abbas and designed the cottages of cob and thatch. Only about forty such cottages were provided, so that the former residents of Milton found themselves crammed together, with as many as four families inhabiting a single cottage. Outwardly Milton Abbas was, as it is today, a place of visual charm, but in the early years of the 'model' village each dwelling must have seethed with bitter resentment.

Overleaf:
The excavated footings of dwellings at the deserted village at Hound Tor, Devon.

The plundering of Milton took place at a time when humanitarian sentiments were beginning to be aroused following the publication of Oliver Goldsmith's poem *The Deserted Village* in 1770:

Sweet smiling village, lovliest of the lawn.
Thy sports are fled, and all thy charms withdrawn;
Amidst thy bowers the tyrant's hand is seen,
And desolation saddens all thy green:
One only master grasps the whole domain,
And half a tillage stints thy smiling plain:
No more thy glassy brook reflects the day,
But chok'd with sedges, works its weedy way.

His supposedly mythical village of 'sweet Auburn' seems to have no other connection with the Auburn swept from the Holderness coast, though it was widely associated with Houghton in Norfolk. Houghton was emparked by Prime Minister Sir Robert Walpole in the 1720s. Recently it has emerged that Goldsmith was probably writing about the emparking of the Oxfordshire village of Newnham. Though only a village, Newnham may have been as populous as Milton. Nevertheless, it was removed by Earl Harcourt because it intruded upon his solitude, and he built the replacement village of Nuneham Courtenay about a mile away. Some old villagers were much less enthusiastic about the move than their master, but the earl apparently employed a poodle poet, William Whitehead, to laud his tender treatment of the villagers.

By Victorian times the crude emparking of villages had become unacceptable to the national community. By this time, however, the showcase of stately homes was almost fully stocked. The lonely church and the lost village site beside it had almost become as much a

Milton Abbas was built to house families evicted from the medieval market town of Milton.

Wimpole Hall in Cambridgeshire commandeered an old village site.

part of the aristocratic setting as the ornamental lake and walled garden. Castle Howard, Harewood, Wimpole, Houghton, Ickworth and Lilford are just a few of the noble mansions which have the corpse of one or more villages for company.

The landscape of the deserted village varied according to the degree of destruction – usually by ploughing – which followed abandonment. Rather than being pulled down with the homes, churches generally disappeared later, most being robbed for valuable building stone. Earthworks that often survive include the hollowed troughs of former streets and lanes, roughly rectangular house plots which may still reveal the platforms where the dwellings themselves stood, and other features associated with the former villages, like Norman motte mounds, embanked fishponds or the moats of old manor houses. As well as the villages which perished completely, there are thousands that have shrunk, but survive. At these places one can see relics of former life; they are an indication of the former extent of the withered settlement.

Right: rethatching one of the Milton Abbas houses, which were once squalid and overcrowded, but are now highly desirable.

Below: Middlesmoor, in Nidderdale, is associated with early Christian worship and the present village grew from a monastic farm.

Opposite: after twice being evicted, the villagers of Wimpole were established in the roadside village of New Wimpole.

7 Landmarks in the village

In the course of their lives most villages have acquired a number of landmarks which punctuate the rows and clusters of dwellings. Some of these landmarks, like churches, are seen in most villages; others, like the remains of market crosses, are found in many, while others still are unique to a particular community or benefactor. Most landmarks have something interesting to tell us about the history of a place and, like the features on a face, they impart character to a village.

Almost invariably, the church is the most historic and important building in a village. It is generally, though falsely, regarded as a glorious symbol of the timeless durability of the settlement. In the development of a village the church in fact undergoes a long sequence of dramatic changes. Churches grew, and sometimes shrank or vanished, according to the pulses in the growth or decline of the congregations which they served. Their layouts, decoration and function all evolved to express changes in belief, ritual and the needs of the community. Today, most village churches are rather cosy and comforting places whereas in the Middle Ages the church was perceived as a place of grandeur which imposed feelings of guilt and awe upon its congregation.

The successive architectural styles can be seen in churches: the Saxon and Norman Romanesque; the Transitional; and the Early English, Decorated and Perpendicular fashions of Gothic architecture. When exploring a church one can expect to recognize building work in two or three of these styles – but it is only when a building and the ground within and outside experience a thorough archaeological excavation that one may realize just how many times a church has

The village lock-up with its conical stone roof on the green at Harrold in Bedfordshire.

126

been rebuilt or remodelled. At Rivenhall in Essex only one twentieth of the area of the churchyard was excavated, but even so the remains of twelve different buildings were exposed, including a Roman villa, a seventeenth-century herring shed, priests' houses and a Saxon church built of timber, while the Saxon stone church which followed experienced five major rebuildings before it reached its nineteenth-century form. The stone Saxon church of the mid-tenth century at Wharram Percy, built on the site of two earlier Saxon churches, went through eight transformations in the next nine centuries. At Hadstock in Essex eight great phases of rebuilding have been recognized. Most of the 18,000 churches maintained by the Church of England are medieval or older, though the histories of all but a select handful are recorded in a very sketchy manner.

A few churches are known to have been attracted to sites sanctified to pagan worship. Fimber Church in Yorkshire was built upon a mound which was originally raised as a Bronze Age barrow and later used for pagan Saxon burials; Rudston Church in Humberside stands beside Britain's tallest ancient monolith, perhaps dragged here over a distance of ten miles and erected during the Bronze Age, and Berwick Church in Sussex was built beside a barrow of the same period.

The fourteenth-century church at Tideswell in Derbyshire has one of the earliest towers in the Perpendicular style and large windows with tracery, reflecting the transition from the Decorated style.

127

Above: the now isolated church at Fawsley in Northamptonshire served two villages which unfortunately lay on the home estate of the arch village destroyers, the Knightley family.

Church of the deserted village of Bawsey, in Norfolk.

Many other village churches are descended from minsters or mother churches which were founded as missionary centres at quite an early stage in the conversion era. But it is probable, as we have seen, that many more originated as places of worship built by local thanes on sites close to their homes, and were originally provided for use by the noble family and their leading retainers. A Saxon law maintained that a man could be considered a thane if he held a certain amount of land and had a church, a kitchen and a place in the king's hall. It is not clear whether most early churches were built in villages or attracted villages to them, but studies in East Anglia have found evidence of pre- and early-Christian settlement in the ground surrounding medieval churches. In some cases the church is known to be a later addition to a village. In the twelfth century it seems to have been a common practice to rip down peasant homes to make way for a church. At the (later deserted) village of Broadfield in Hertfordshire, peasant properties were destroyed when the church was built early in the thirteenth century and the street plan of the village was changed to align the main street with the church.

Every village church has a dedication, which sometimes contains hints of early worship. In Buckinghamshire, St Laurence dedications are linked to Roman settlements and might suggest a continuity of worship since Roman times. In the same county St Leonard dedications seem to be related to both Roman sites and ancient woodland, perhaps underlining the link between the Christian saint and the Celtic hunter-god, Cernunnos. Throughout England St Michael dedications are widely associated with pagan hilltop sites and this may reveal a connection between the archangel and those pagan gods that guarded and escorted the dead. In Cornwall there are many churches dedicated to obscure Celtic saints who are believed to have brought Christianity to the locality concerned. The roads to the shrine of the Virgin at Walsingham are punctuated by churches dedicated to St Mary, whose cult following developed during the twelfth century.

Most of the more venerable churches have grown from humble beginnings. Originally there may have been only a preaching cross, where a priest from the nearest minster would conduct an open-air village service and perform baptisms. Burials would be made in the surrounding ground, which was sanctified by the presence of the cross, while the next stage involved the provision of a building to shelter the worshippers, often a simple wooden structure consisting of a nave for the congregation and a chancel enclosing the altar where the priest performed the sacraments. The small, rustic churches of the Saxon era were generally rebuilt within a few generations of their creation to allow for the growth in congregations.

In the thirteenth century village populations were still swelling with great vigour. As a result south and then north aisles were added to many churches. Changes were also taking place in church ritual, which became more elaborate. Apses were often added during the Norman era but then obliterated during later rebuildings, for, in the thirteenth century, chancels were often enlarged to accommodate more impressive ceremonial displays and to increase the isolation between the priest and the worshippers. Late in the Middle Ages rood screens were added to emphasize this separation, though after the Reformation almost all of them were destroyed. Another reason for the expansion of churches was that, in the later part of the Middle Ages, most monastic orders were perceived as avaricious and dissolute and benefactors tended to endow their local churches rather than the monasteries that had benefited previously. The money was used to add side chapels where masses could be said for patrons, both wealthy individuals or members of the trade guild concerned.

The experience of going to church was very different for villagers in the Middle Ages from the one we have today. It was one which gradually evolved, but around the time of Magna Carta (1215) the members of the congregation would probably have approached a building which did not have the hue of time-mellowed stone but which was lime-washed and gleaming white like a huge architectural glacier. As they entered the great south doorway, they dipped their grimy fingers into a stoup at the threshold and crossed themselves with holy water. The interior of the village church was also lime-washed, yet still very dark, and instead of painted glass, the window openings were covered in canvas blinds. Only when their eyes had become accustomed to the gloom could the worshippers admire the gaudy paintwork outlining the door and window openings. There were other paintings which emphasized the vivid dramas of the world to come and which contrasted with the dour austerity of day-to-day life. On the chancel arch there was a chilling representation of the Resurrection and Last Judgment, and standing on a tie beam above was the Great Rood, a carving of Christ crucified but victorious, flanked by the figures of Mary and John.

In contrast to the churches of today, those of the thirteenth century seemed barn-like and empty. The dusty earthen floor was strewn with rushes, but it was otherwise bare except for a great timber chest and the font, which was barred and locked to prevent the hallowed water being filched for use in witchcraft. There were no pews, although the old and ailing members of the congregation could

The isolated church in the park at Ickworth marks the site of Ickworth's lost village.

Overleaf:
Ickworth Hall was built by the 4th Earl of Bristol after 1795 in a park already depopulated by the removal of the village.

lean against the walls or sometimes rest on stone benches set around them. Neither was there a pulpit. In the fifteenth century many village churches gained their first pulpit and pews following the adoption of a popular fashion for preaching initiated by the friars, who were admired more than other monks and clergy.

By the fifteenth century the village church had experienced profound changes. Gone were the slit-like windows and canvas blinds. In their place came large traceried windows filled with pageants in coloured or stained glass. The building of new aisles and of clerestoreys had been accompanied by the insertion of windows in the larger and more ornate Decorated and Perpendicular styles. Church interiors were still brightly painted with murals, which were often more garish than devout, covering most of the available wall space. The adoption of preaching during services did not narrow the gap between the congregation and the clergy. Indeed, the separation of nave and chancel by an ornately carved rood screen left the villagers as mere onlookers, while the clergy in peacock vestments celebrated the Mass.

Although the central rituals of the church were no less mysterious than they had been centuries earlier, the church was also the focus of more down-to-earth pleasures. The nave was the responsibility of the parish, the symbol of the Church Militant, the nearest medieval equivalent to a village hall and also the venue for boisterous parties or church ales. Miracle plays were performed in the nave, but only the drama of the discovery of Christ's empty tomb could be re-enacted in the chancel. As well as executing the esoteric aspects of religion, the medieval church was also expected to attend to more pressing concerns – like ensuring a harvest and blessing the plough.

Few village churches were built in the centuries after the Reformation, although by Victorian times much rebuilding and restoration was necessary. By the end of the Middle Ages most villages had a church large enough for the congregation. As a result of the Reformation the church became a place for services rather than a mystical palace for ritual. The buildings survived, but their interiors were gutted and, some would say, vandalized. Out went the Great Roods, rood screens, relics, altars, coloured glass, wall paintings, shrines and statues. Most of what was missed by the zealots of Edward VI's reign was smashed by those of Elizabeth's or by militant Puritans. Communion tables appeared in the place of altars and stark biblical texts were painted on whitened walls which had formerly been alive with murals.

As the years rolled by, the quantity and quality of Christian worship in the community came to depend upon the two pillars of

Village churches were once alive with painted decoration, but little has survived time, iconoclasm and restoration. Above: a twelfth-century wall-painting of the Descent from the Cross at Easby, near Richmond, Yorkshire. Right: the Archangel Michael, 1493, on a rood screen which depicts saints and kings at Ludham, Norfolk.

Overleaf: Medieval village congregations were surrounded by a pageant of wall-paintings. Few survive, but at Little Missenden in Buckinghamshire, murals of the fourteenth century were rediscovered in the 1930s and restored.

At Steeple Ashton, Wiltshire, the pinnacled south aisle (in the foreground) was paid for by a local clothier, William Leucas, in the late fifteenth century.

the village establishment, the squire and the parson. The resolute squire would ensure that the parish was not served by a wastrel or a bore and would make sure that his own family, servants and as many tenants as possible filled the pews. While religious images and statuary had been removed in the Reformation, the church then became packed with monuments to the squire's forbears – and in many villages the church resembled a family mausoleum more than a place of communal worship. The nave was filled with rows of pews, but the inequalities in village society were underlined by the seating arrangements. The squire had the best pew and in some places he had his own gallery – complete with fireplace in a few churches. Worship now focused not on obscure but impressive ritual but on the sermon, delivered from the elevated heights of the pulpit and imposing in its length if not its content. At the west end of the church there was often a gallery containing a small choir and a village band, who struggled through the heavy musical diet of psalms.

If the village church underwent changes in the course of time, it also varied from region to region. A vast Suffolk village church of the fifteenth century would look completely out of place serving a Cornish hamlet. This incongruity would not only be a matter of size and opulence but also a case of the building materials and architectural features jarring with the setting. Some regional variations are easily explained because they concern the availability of materials – there is

In the late medieval period East Anglia was among the richest areas of England and its churches were rebuilt on a lavish scale. One of the grandest is that of Long Melford, in Suffolk; the eastern chapels use elaborate flushwork panelling in stone and flint.

all the difference in the world between Cornish granite, Suffolk flint and the limestone of the Cotswolds. Others are related to local preferences and idiosyncrasies and can be impossible to rationalize, as for example the enthusiasm in medieval East Midlands for broach spires. Then there are the accidents of history which permit one community to grow large and rich and acquire a church to match or allowed a wealthy benefactor to have been born in a particular place.

The original Saxon churches were often made of timber. Just one example, much altered, survives at Greensted in Essex. For the first few medieval centuries – and for much longer in some places – the church was the only stone building in the village. Roads were poor and transport costs prohibitive, so that while high-grade building stone from other regions or from Normandy might be imported for great cathedral works, churches were normally built of the material which was to hand. In the chalk country builders were reduced to setting flint nodules in a matrix of mortar. In Cornwall they struggled to hew blocks from great slabs of granite moorstone. But in other places, like Northamptonshire, Gloucestershire or parts of Dorset, the creamy limestones were all that the quarrymen and mason could desire. Necessity often required the use of low-grade stones for the main fabric of the village church and in such cases tougher or more workable grades were imported to form the quoins and window and door surrounds. In general it can be said that most

One of the best surviving Saxon preaching crosses is at Irton, in Cumbria.

Right: a rare example of a Norman village church with a twin-gabled tower is at Fingest, in the Chilterns.

The unspoilt church at Barfrestone, Kent, is small but renowned for its carved decoration (see p. 51), probably accomplished in the twelfth century by craftsmen working on the cathedrals of Canterbury or Rochester.

village churches had their origins in a quarry site which would have been visible from their towers.

In modern England ill-judged campaigns of renewal are making each provincial city centre look just like every other one. In the villages, however, old churches survive to proclaim the vitality and unpredictability of regional taste. The expressions of this are far too numerous to list, but they include the towers with stair turrets in south Devon, the ornate 'sound holes' in the towers of some Norfolk churches, the lack of clerestoreys in the southern strip of England, the hammerbeam roofs of East Anglia and the wagon roofs of the South West. Local preferences can prove impossible to explain, although in some cases masons and carpenters must have imitated features seen at the great building sites in their neighbourhood; in this way several village churches in the vicinity of Lincoln have ornate piers which mimic those of the cathedral. When medieval masons were contracted to build a church at Walberswick in Suffolk, they were told to imitate the tower of Tunstall Church and the west door and windows from Halesworth.

The medieval churchyard was, in its different ways, both a pleasant and a macabre place. Graves were relatively shallow and, as relatives of the dead could not always afford coffins, the deceased was buried in shrouds or even old clothes. Tombstones were never considered, so that it was much easier to chase and frolic across the open, bumpy surface. Any preaching cross which preceded the building of the church would have been lost or incorporated into the fabric during any rebuilding, though during the Middle Ages many new crosses were erected in association with Palm Sunday processions. Members of the congregation processed from the north door behind a plain, draped cross which was exchanged for a jewelled cross at the last station in the churchyard as a symbol of the risen Christ.

The excavation of churchyards at places like Wharram Percy and Aldwark, York, has produced interesting information about medieval people. They were not as short as has been assumed; men averaged a height of 5 feet 5 inches (1.69 metres) and women 5 feet 1 inch (1.57 metres), but their lifespans were considerably less than ours. At Wharram it was thought that only one person in ten reached the age of 50, with the average lifespan being 35 years for men and 31 for women. (Recent scientific evidence seems to suggest, however, that these figures may be severe underestimates.)

Access to the churchyard may be gained via a lych gate, often a gabled roof supported on piers of oak. The structure may appear venerable but most lych gates are less than three centuries old. In

Walberswick, in Suffolk, was rebuilt in the fifteenth century (the masons were told to copy the tower of one neighbouring church and the windows of another) but it proved too large and with the decay of the village the church was shortened.

medieval times the churchyard was frequently approached via a stile, beside which a long slab of stone lay where the body was placed to await the priest. Lych gates were provided to offer shelter to bearers and mourners as they waited with the corpse to be received into the sanctified area. At Bolney in Sussex an old coffin stone on a plinth stands beneath the gable of the lych gate. One of the oldest surviving lych gates is at Ashwell in Hertfordshire; it is thought to date from the fifteenth century.

Close to the churchyard one may expect to find the village vicarage. In a few places its medieval precursor, the priest's house, survives. There is a fine thatched example dating from the late medieval period at Muchelney in Somerset, while the foundations of older buildings have been found during churchyard excavations. Old vicarages reflect the affluence of the parish and many were built to accommodate a small contingent of servants and allow lavish entertainment. Where the squire controlled the advowson or right to appoint a minister, the successful candidate was often a relative or a prospective husband for the daughter of the squire – so that certain standards of comfort had to be maintained. Modern incumbents may struggle to heat an over-large residence on an under-large stipend, while the church authorities lurk in the wings waiting to sell the house and grounds to developers. The current tendency to amalgamate parishes has led to the decommissioning of countless vicarages and has severed the centuries-old bonds of contact between priest and parish.

Stocks were another important feature of village life. These symbols of public humiliation survive in a number of places, like Budworth in Cheshire, the market square at Ripley in Yorkshire and in the

Whitened on the outside but dark within, the early medieval church was an awe-inspiring building. Refenestration opened up most window spaces, but at Stewkley in Buckinghamshire (above) the slit-like Norman windows still survive.

Hubberholme in the Yorkshire Dales (above right) was so remote that it escaped a command banning rood-lofts. The loft itself, used for musicians, was brought from Coverham Abbey after the Dissolution in 1548.

Right: the palatial church at Patrington near Hull was built in the Decorated style until work was halted by the Black Death. It was finished in 1410 in the Perpendicular style.

churchyard at Ottery St Mary in Devon. The survivors are unlikely to be of original medieval vintage; while stocks have been in use since at least the start of the thirteenth century, they continued to be repaired and used until Victorian times. The medieval portfolio of remedies for anti-social behaviour also included pillories, cucking stools and ducking stools. Whipping posts were other manifestations of the barbarous side of old village life and a few examples still stand, as at Stow in Lincolnshire and Aldbury in Hertfordshire.

Village lock-ups are more common and reflect the rough-and-ready nature of rural justice. Before the organization of police forces, law and order was the responsibility of the village constable, who needed somewhere to confine wrongdoers until they could be handed over to a higher authority – and probably also a place where local drunks could be left to sleep off their ills. The lock-ups that were built frequently survive, though many are humdrum little buildings which might be mistaken for brick sheds or privies. Sometimes an existing structure was commandeered, like the south porch of Stratton Church in Cornwall, though occasionally a more imposing gaol was built, like the stone cylinder at Castle Cary in Somerset with its helmet-like roof, dating from 1779.

The agricultural equivalent of the lock-up was the pinfold or pound. A pound must have existed on almost every medieval manor and was used to impound livestock which had trespassed on neighbouring property. The lord of the manor maintained the pound and a village official, the pinder, was responsible for arresting the offending beasts. In consequence he was doubtless reviled and abused by the remainder of the community until one or other of its members found a stray grazing on his corn. During the Middle Ages, when the widespread nature of open field farming made pounds an essential feature of rural life, most pinfolds would have been gated enclosures framed by walls, palings or thick hedges. Aspects of open field farming survived in some localities until Victorian times and some of the later village pounds still exist, like the fine brick structure at Raskelf in Yorkshire, with its battlements and barred Gothic windows and door, while at Hutton-le-Hole near Pickering the pound is circular and of stone.

With the decline in attendances at church, the village school has frequently become the centre of communal life, so that the loss of the school is seen as a calamity for the village. Many schools are Victorian buildings and legacies of the Act of 1870, which made public funds available for schooling. In medieval times such village education as existed was provided by the church, and later schooling relied upon charitable donations. By Georgian times schools of one kind or another were to be found in about half the villages of England. Many of the old schools were dame schools presided over by women – often spinsters – who lacked any special teaching qualifications or facilities. In quite small villages the locals may be able to point to two or three houses which accommodated such schools at different times.

When village education depended upon patronage, it reflected the values of these patrons. Generally it was considered unwise to provide children with any more than basic numeracy and literacy, so that they would not aspire to ambitions above their station. Parents who relied upon the pennies that their children could earn from tasks like stone picking and bird scaring and village worthies who needed child labour at key times in the farming calendar all ensured that absentee rates were high in the village school.

Like the school and the church, the village inn seems to be an almost timeless institution. However, until the eighteenth century, the greater part of the ale consumed in the village was brewed at home. When one explores the inventories which were commonly drawn up to itemize the possessions of dead villagers, the paraphernalia of brewing features almost as frequently as beds and stools. In the medieval village beer brewed for sale was made by various alewives in small and scarcely modified houses and the product was then tested by the official taster. The village sometimes contained a tavern, but if it did, the inn would be a rather squalid and poorly appointed place, its sign no more than a pole or a bush hanging at the door.

The manor controlled brewing by appointing the aletaster. It also regulated the building of inns and the conversion of houses. The national enthusiasm for ale was a lucrative source of fines and the medieval manor court rolls show that women were the main

The Saxon and Norman round towers of East Anglia churches, like Roydon in Norfolk, are thought to reflect the difficulties of making sharp corners in flint.

Village pubs can display local history. At Gisburn in the forest of Bowland, both reveal the influence of the Lords Ribblesdale, the local overlords. There is the Ribblesdale Arms and also the White Bull, alluding to the white cattle kept in the local manor park.

offenders – on the retailing side at least. In 1384 Cecilia de Thorne of Methley near Wakefield was fined for various brewing offences, including not displaying a sign or 'alestake', and in 1413 Alice del Milne of Hipperholme, also in Yorkshire, was fined for brewing and making a new alehouse. A Methley by-law of 1498 demanded that every brewer in the lordship should display an 'ailswispe' or alestake before her door and that every brewer should provide a bed for a guest. In a few villages the local enthusiasm for ale is still constrained by manorial controls, and Ripley near Harrogate has just regained a pub after a drought lasting more than two generations, imposed by a master who did not share the villagers' taste for ale. However, there are many other villages where the pub is named after the armorial bearings of the family of the squire.

Medieval records show that from at least the thirteenth century onwards inns were quite numerous, but they seem to have been much more common in villages which stood near a busy highway. In the post-medieval centuries inns proliferated and villages which may now boast just one or two often supported four or five times as many. Pub names were changed with careless abandon, so that while some, like the Drovers' or the Devonshire Arms, may tell us about former clients or estate connections, many just reflect the whimsical choices of former landlords. Inns were sufficiently numerous in the Middle Ages to attract periodical condemnation by the church.

Writing in 1652, the unidentified 'S.T.' calculated that England contained about 100,000 alehouses, of which at least 8000 were in rural settings. He blamed an excess of alehouses for the corruption of the population:

Should I begin with Gentlemen of very good Families, who make it their only business to sit piping and potting all the day, nay all the week, the year, nay their life; and when their estate will not bear the Tavern, or Inns in Towns, yet they may be found in some smoky blind Alehouse, if it be no more than a Cott of turf against a tree on some Common . . . And who doth not see the Country-Husbandman (in whose labour consists the welfare of the Commonwealth) spend more time in these pestilent Alehouses than he doth on the plough, and oft times runs so far on the score that he runs himself out of all, and then he, his wife and children must beg.

8 The village homes

To the native the village is a place of friends, relatives and neighbours, but to the stranger it is primarily a collection of buildings. The dwellings are not like those seen in towns: they differ in the ways in which they are built, the patterns and groupings that they form and in the manner in which they are much more expressive of their region and its character. The rough masons, carpenters and home-makers of village England may seldom have given a thought to the aesthetic aspects of their creations and yet, in village after village, they produced a prettiness in which romance and sentiment could become deeply rooted. In stark contrast, the highly qualified architects, developers and planners of the modern age seem hardly ever to be able to produce additions to villages which do other than scar the face of the settlement. To appreciate the dwellings of the old village, we must seek to understand how they were built, what purposes they were expected to serve and how the changes in the way of life demanded modifications to the layout and to the ways in which living space was used.

Firstly, however, we must discover how the short-lived and tumbledown hovels of the medieval village gave way to the homes which lasted for centuries. We have already seen something of the evolution of village dwellings, such as the sunken huts and halls of the Dark Ages and the widely adopted medieval long-house, but these were not truly durable structures and they can only be glimpsed in the form of modern reconstructions. At Askham in Yorkshire in 1295 a farmer was sued for pulling down three cottages which belonged to Bridlington Priory. The prior had valued the three dwellings at a mere pound. In the values of the 1930s, when a

Local stone, thatch and unpretentious design produced houses that never lose their appeal: Pilton, Northamptonshire, c. 1700.

Overleaf: Almshouses and windmill at Thaxted, Essex.

respectable cottage could be bought for around £200, the trio would have been worth about £7 – and this helps to reveal just how impoverished most of the earlier medieval peasant dwellings really were.

It is certainly the case that a good number of villages contain houses which incorporate sections of building dating from the fifteenth and even the fourteenth centuries, but these more solid buildings were not the homes of the peasant majority – they belonged to wealthy tradesmen, clothiers and merchants. For the yeoman families and the more affluent tenant farmers to be rehoused in a manner in which their forbears may never have dreamed, a complete change of outlook was needed. This change was embodied in a movement now known as the Great Rebuilding. It was identified and given its name by a great pioneer of landscape studies, Professor W. G. Hoskins. Concentrating mainly on southern England, Professor Hoskins dated the movement to the period 1570–1640. The movement began in the pace-setting south-east rather earlier than suggested and spread slowly into the less affluent backwaters, so that in the north it was a phenomenon of Georgian times. With its origins in the late Tudor and Elizabethan decades, the Great Rebuilding was based upon widespread aspirations for self-improvement and was rooted in agricultural prosperity, lively commerce and a sense of security deriving from relatively strong and stable government.

New dwellings erupted like mushrooms in the autumn mists to accommodate the growing population. Not all of them were desirable or desired and an ineffectual act of 1589 attempted to ban the building of any cottage which did not stand in a holding of at least four acres and to prevent more than one family from occupying a home; it complained of the 'erection of great numbers of cottages which are daily more increased in many parts of this Realme'. An example was the small parish of Epworth in Lincolnshire, which gained a hundred new dwellings in the last quarter of the sixteenth century. When researching the modest Cambridgeshire village of Foxton, Rowland Parker found that between 1550 and 1620 the village was rebuilt, with more than fifty new dwellings arising on derelict sites. These dwellings were not shanties or hovels: their oak-braced walls were so solid that twenty examples are still standing. The families who provided the impetus for this revolution in Foxton were not those long established in the village but were immigrants from neighbouring villages who injected new vitality into the place – a factor which seems to have quickened the pace of change in other villages too.

All this activity was unrestrained by planners or building regulations and the manor courts were kept busy fining those who had illegally felled timber, quarried the roads for chalk and rubble or allowed their new homes to obtrude upon the highway. Although little evidence remains, it would seem that much of the timber-framed building work in the Elizabethan village was accomplished by the prospective occupants, with help from friends and relations. Carpenters, whose skills must have been in great demand, may have cut the joints in the prefabricated frames and bricklayers would have been hired to make chimneys.

A careful study of the houses erected during the Great Rebuilding in the Dorset village of Yetminster was made by R. Machin. This village was in an area of dairy farming in the seventeenth century and it emerged from the evidence of the datestones that the farmers tended to build substantial houses for their families after periods of two or more years when the prices for pastoral products had been high and that of the grain which they had to purchase had been low. The tenants here had the right to take timber from the manor to build or repair dwellings and to hew stone from local quarries for the same purposes. Similar rights existed on many other manors and the ability to obtain free building materials greatly favoured the home-maker.

Even so, house building was a costly affair, one which consumed the savings of several years as well as additional finance in the form of loans from fellow villagers. The Yetminster area had a tradition of stone building. In the sixteenth century stone dwellings were more costly to erect than timber-framed houses – though in the next century timber prices rose sharply. In 1679 a stone house in Yetminster with two storeys, including a hall, bakehouse and buttery on the ground floor, could be built for about £60. This outlay would include the wages of craftsmen, paid at a rate of about 12d. (5p) a day, and of labourers paid at two-thirds of this rate. It seems that a well-built village house cost around the equivalent of four years' earnings by a joiner or mason – more or less the levels prevailing in modern England before the worst excesses of the property boom of the 1980s.

The exteriors of Yetminster houses still appear much as they did when newly built. The interiors, however, are drastically different. Though not as barren of furniture as the medieval peasant home, the village dwelling of Elizabethan and Stuart times looked nothing like even the most antique-ridden cottage of today. Our ideas about the purposes of rooms have changed greatly. For a start, most people in the old villages were farmers or farmworkers, while many who had

*Opposite:
This cottage at
Rockbourne, in
Hampshire, epitomizes
our visions of the village
home. Old bricks in
irregular courses infill the
square panels of the light
framing timber.*

*The hazards of tourism: a
new shop-front and an
over-provision of signs
detract from the charm of
Cockington, in Devon.*

*Left: a village landscape
in local stone at
Clapham, in the
Yorkshire Dales.*

other occupations also kept a few sheep, cattle or pigs and perhaps a nag. Consequently, homes were full of the paraphernalia of farming, milking, brewing and the processing and storing of freshly killed or harvested farm produce. Whereas today we think of a home in terms of a lounge, kitchen, bedrooms, study, bathroom and so on, the rooms in a typical Yetminster village dwelling of 1668 were listed as follows: the hall, which was the main living-room; the buttery, packed with ten barrels; the milkhouse, with its butter tub, cheese vats and cheese press; the hall chamber, serving as a bedroom; and the cheese loft, which was used as a second bedroom. By Elizabethan times all but the poorest villagers had beds and bedding and some had feather mattresses. But beds tended to be found in what we would regard as the most unlikely corners. The cheese loft of one Yetminster farm of 1707 contained a bed and thirty-six cheeses and there was also a feather bed in the kitchen chamber.

What may seem to our eyes to be domestic anarchy also prevailed in the north of the country. We can learn this through studying inventories that were compiled when country people died. William Coates was a blacksmith of Burnt Yates hamlet near Harrogate. When he died in 1673, the contents of his purse and his apparel were valued at £1 15s. 4d. (about £1.77 in today's money) and his accounts showed that he was owed 18s. 4d. (about 92p). His 'house' or hall contained two tables but, strangely, only one chair, a cupboard, a chest, a brass pot, a kettle and four pieces of pewter. In the adjoining parlour there were a bed and bedclothes, a chest, a coffer, three stools and a trough for making dough, while the small chamber housed another bed and a cradle. A modest set of work tools, some coal and a pile of logs lay in the smithy and there were three hens and six chicks in the yard.

A neighbour, James Kilvington, died in 1678. He was evidently a small tenant farmer and linen worker, for his inventory shows that he kept a flock of 30 sheep, had 20 cattle of various ages, a mare, a nag, a foal and a stock of fodder as well as a store of cloth. Again we find the home cluttered with the paraphernalia of living, working, sleeping and food processing. The main living-room contained two tables, consisting of boards and frames, three chairs, three buffet stools and a bench, a candlestick, shelves stacked with pewter, sides of beef and bacon, two spits and tongs and a great jumble of cheese-making equipment, including 45 milk bowls. In the parlour there were a cupboard, another frame table, a chest, a bedstead and bedding, 34 yards of hemp and linen cloth that James had woven and some butter-making and brewing equipment: two churns, four tubs,

The interior of a late fifteenth-century merchant's house from Bromsgrove rebuilt at the Avoncroft Museum of Buildings, showing the steps from the hall to the private sitting room and sleeping loft above. The structure is of timber, the walls of wattle covered in clay.

two barrels and a bottle. Dairying also intruded into the small third chamber, where there were three beds and bedding and four large cheeses.

The Great Rebuilding was a mixture of revolution and evolution. The medieval long-house had only one room, or at best a passageway and wattle screen to separate the family and its beasts. In the far west and the north-east of England one-roomed dwellings, often roofed in turf, could still be found in Victorian times. In the south-east dwellings with two storeys had been the norm for almost three centuries. The village long-house was superseded in the more prosperous parts of the south and east by the two-roomed cottage home well before the end of the Middle Ages. Livestock were excluded from the house, which now consisted of a hall or living-room with a hearth, and a chamber or bower, used mainly for sleeping. At first smoke from the hearth still drifted around the open rafters, windows had canvas blinds but no glass and all the dramas of family life were enacted upon rush-strewn floors of trampled earth.

Early in the sixteenth century lofts reached by ladders were inserted into southern village homes and provided extra sleeping and storage space. This move led to single-storey dwellings being converted into homes with upper floors and wooden staircases, and

Overleaf:
Upper left: close studding displayed in the medieval village guildhouse of Whittlesford in Cambridgeshire. Bottom left and opposite: the Great Rebuilding preserved in the landscape of Elstow in Bedfordshire.

new houses were then built to this popular layout. Extra space could also be obtained by lengthening the dwelling and adding an additional bay to create third or fourth rooms at ground-floor level, with others above. It was easier to elongate a peasant dwelling than to add cross wings in the manner adopted by the rich.

In areas where timber framing was used, the dwelling had its main structure formed by pairs of posts set in line. Sometimes houses were described in this manner, as in a survey of Ripley in North Yorkshire of 1635:

John Cooke: house of 3 pairs of posts, 2 parlours, 2 chambers; and a barn of 2 pairs of posts, one other barn of 2 pairs of posts £1 6s. 8d. [£1.33 rent]. William Craven: house of 5 pairs of posts, the timber is in great decay, a barn in the north end of the house 16s. 8d. [82p rent].

This entry shows that the Craven family now had a wall between themselves and their livestock, with the animals being kept in a barn at the north end of the house. The survey reveals that it was now common in the locality for barns to be built on the low or downslope ends of dwellings. As the Great Rebuilding exerted its greatest influence in the northern dales during the eighteenth century, so the old traditions of long-house building and timber framing were replaced by the building of 'laithe-houses' in stone. Village farmsteads of this type were often built two storeys tall and a solid wall separated the domestic quarters from the adjoining byre.

Several other changes increased the comforts of cottage life. Perhaps the most important was the adoption of chimneys and fireplaces to replace the smoke hole at the top of the roof gable and the hearth which smouldered in the centre of the room. At first wattle and daub funnels and smoke hoods served as chimneys, but in Elizabethan times safer and more serviceable chimneys of brick or stone were built against the end wall of the hall. Most cooking was now done here rather than in any purpose-built kitchen, with spits, pot hooks and pot cranes standing and hanging in the broad fireplace opening and with a bread oven built into the wall beside the fireplace. In the middle of the seventeenth century the most affluent villagers in the south-eastern counties were beginning to adopt windows with small glazed panes to replace the shutters and canvas screens and provide a less draughty form of ventilation. Floors remained primitive, the earth being dug up and removed when it became fouled by domestic waste. Sometimes blood and mud were mixed to form a coating for the earth. Eventually flagstones and tiles were accepted as a more hygienic form of flooring.

With smoke streaming from its brick chimney, little panes twinkling in the ground-floor windows and in the dormers inserted above and the livestock now evicted to the byre, the seventeenth-century village home was outwardly beginning to match our perceptions of 'olde worlde' life. Inside, however, it remained a different story. No villager would have had the remotest idea of what either a bathroom or a bath was. For all but the very richest the lavatory was at best a pit and a boarded privy above. Water still came not from pipes or a kitchen pump but in a bucket from a communal well or spring – and there will have been scarcely a village in the land which could not be smelt as soon as it was seen.

The old way of life, with its domestic clutter, intimate contact and its intermeshing of work and home life, was a product of its time. Villagers seldom visited shops and the range of goods for sale at market stalls was small. Much or most food was home-produced. There was no public transport and only the better-off families could afford to support a riding horse. The mother would probably have spent the day hauling water, stoking the fire and tending the family's few sheep, cattle and poultry. When the children returned exhausted from work on a neighbouring farm, they would be despatched to gather more fuel. The father would return from his farm work at dusk and rinse his hands and face in the rain butt. After a stew of home-grown produce, mother and father would resume work, one perhaps spinning and the other weaving, eyes straining in the candlelight to earn the extra pennies needed to pay the rent. And then, as likely as not, the whole family would retire to a single chamber and sleep in their work clothes.

Public health and other facilities scarcely existed. The roads approaching and traversing the village were vile, for neither manor nor parish could marshal the resources or authority to keep them maintained. There was no system for sewage or for water supply, with the result that the two mingled and merged. Perhaps the depths of unsociability were plumbed in 1386 when the abbot of Chertsey allowed two cavernous wells to exist on the road between Staines and Egham in Surrey; when a traveller fell down one of them and drowned the abbot did not consider awarding any compensation but instead laid claim to the goods of the victim. Of course, the villagers themselves could have done much more to improve their collective lot. In fact, they seem to have done very little. It is ironic that communities plainly capable of running the most intricate systems of co-operative farming appear to have been quite indifferent to the squalor at their own doorsteps. Instead, the old records tell of

Close studding in the former inn at Swaffham Bulbeck, in Cambridgeshire.

Decorative plasterwork or pargetting on the priest's house of 1473 at Clare, in Suffolk.

middens encroaching upon the streets and streams of drinking water which were fouled and obstructed despite all the vain exhortations of the manor courts.

In the Middle Ages such charity that did exist was provided by the church. Under the Act of Settlement of 1662 paupers became eligible for some support from their parish of birth or residence. The effect of this, however, was to reduce, rather than to increase, the amount of low-cost housing available. The landowners who were taxed to raise the poor rate often sought to reduce their dues by allowing cottages to decay or even by tearing them down. By doing so, they removed the niches where paupers could settle. The inhumanity of the haves towards the have-nots is exemplified by a story related at the start of the eighteenth century by the yeoman Richard Gough in his *History of Myddle*, a parish in Shropshire.

He tells how Humphrey Beddow, a lame shoemaker, came to work in the parish and married a local girl. Soon the village worthies were complaining that he might become a burden on them. Meanwhile Humphrey fell ill, though he promised to return to his native parish as soon as he recovered. The illness was long and it robbed him of his business. He was despatched from Myddle to his own parish of Cardington. However, the pillars of Cardington life did not want him back, claiming that Humphrey had 'procured a settlement' in Myddle by virtue of his forty days' residence. With a lack of Christian goodwill so characteristic of many of the more fortunate people of his day, Gough boasted: 'This was the first contest that wee had and thus wee lost it; but thanks be to God wee never lost any afterwards.'

Most of those village vistas that we cherish are largely the products of that massive surge of vitality, the Great Rebuilding. The dwellings that have survived to this day, mainly homes of some substance built for families of some wealth, give a most unbalanced picture of life and landscape as they existed two or three centuries ago. Not every villager could live in this way; we do not see the hovels which perished long ago. Gone are the shanties of mud, sticks and straw which harboured the paupers – or which were torn down because they might harbour them. Gone too are most of the commons and the huts and hovels of turf of the squatter communities who lived in filth and ran a few cows on the open grazings. The period houses in today's village are costly and gentrified. We do not see them as some were, partitioned and partitioned again to accommodate as many hungry landworkers as their walls would hold. Nor do we see the cottages which were tied to a particular estate or farm and which were inhabited by cowering families who knew that the merest insubordinate mutter or cringing appeal for better wages could spell instant eviction and pauperhood.

Through the eyes of fiction and fancy we see the old village as a bastion of community. In reality 'olde worlde' village society was riven by class consciousness and the village home symbolized the family status or lack of same. The tyranny of class did not end at the church door, for status determined whether one sat at the front of the congregation on a pew of privilege or stood at the back with the reeking masses. As Gough explained: 'A pew or seat does not belong to a person or to land, butt to an house, therefore, if a man remove from an house to dwell in another, hee shall not retaine the seat belonging to the first house.'

Fierce tensions existed between the different classes in village society. The state provided no security, the courts little justice and every householder feared those quirks of misfortune which could propel the family downwards into a lower social rank. This insecurity may partly explain the cruel contempt displayed to those at the bottom of village society. Fecklessness, drink and the survival of rights to the common were all proclaimed as the causes of poverty by those more favoured by fortune. In the old village the yeoman looked up to the squire, the tenant farmer looked up to the yeoman, the day labourer to the tenant – and all looked down on the weak and the jobless. Daniel Defoe was no more reactionary than most others of his class, but on encountering the family of a Derbyshire lead miner surviving on 8d. (3p) a day and having a cave as their only home, he remarked that their abode was superior to '. . . the dirt and nastiness of the miserable cottages of the poor, though many of them spend more in strong drink than this poor woman had to maintain five children with.'

Very few of the humbler home-makers in the old village gave a thought to the outward appearances of their cottages or farmsteads. Function and cost determined the structure of the home. Lifestyle and tradition decided the layout and function of rooms, while the main economic factor concerned the availability of building materials. The wonderful vernacular architecture of the English villages owes a great deal to the terrible state of the roads of the realm. In 1726 Defoe wrote about the great improvements made to the great national highway of Watling Street, but when John Wesley travelled the same road about a decade later he found that: 'The rain continued all the way to Dunstable, where we exchanged the main road for the fields, which, having just been ploughed, were deep enough.' At this time there was scarcely a main road in England in as good a

Overleaf:
The honey coloured stone of the Cotswolds in buildings at Lower Slaughter, in Gloucestershire.

condition as it had been in Roman times. As a result, goods tended to be transported by river boats and pack horse teams. Building materials were bulky and unwieldy and, since they could not bear the added costs of transport, they were obtained locally. Before the days of the railway each village had developed an architectural identity founded on the timber, clay and stone resources of its setting.

A particular district might be rich in woodland but poor in stone, and in such a place one would expect to find the tradition of timber-framed buildings continuing until such time as its hardwood forestry industry collapsed or faced impossible competition from locally made or imported bricks. The use of massive oak timbers and of sill beams raised above the damp ground on footings of rubble or brick allowed the construction of dwellings which could last indefinitely. Although many villagers had the right to take building timber on the manor, most of the better houses were built of timbers felled in a commercially organized wood, prefabricated by a carpenter as shaped but unseasoned beams, studs and braces, and then assembled on the building site according to the guide numbers inscribed on each component by the craftsman.

Two different techniques existed, sometimes side by side. The cruck-framing tradition had each bay of a house or barn bracketed by 'A'-shaped frames or crucks, each cruck being formed of two long, curving blades of oak which were joined at their apices to form a gable. Though quite widely used in parts of the north and west, the size of a house built in this way was restricted, both in terms of height and width, by the length of substantial timbers available. Cruck framing is still displayed in some bijou dwellings in the West Midlands, while in the northern dales many such frames are rendered invisible by encasing walls of stone.

Most of the modest cottages and farmsteads built in the cruck manner have perished and many times more examples of the alternative, box-framing, technique survive. By building rigid boxes composed of horizontal beams, upright studs and posts and diagonal braces all mortised together, it was possible to create anything from a cramped cottage to a mansion with long ranges and several wings. Within this almost universal tradition several distinctive regional variations evolved. Much about the old village dwellings can be explained in terms of tradition and practical expediency, but, as with churches, there are some regional preferences which defy such simple analysis. In and beyond East Anglia a form of box framing known as 'close studding' was favoured, the walls of the dwellings being framed in upright posts or studs set close together. In the

Square panel framing in the style of the West Midlands at Weobley, Hereford and Worcester.

eastern counties this tradition seems to have begun by the thirteenth century and it persisted until the decline of timber framing after the seventeenth century. In Tudor and Elizabethan times close studding was particularly popular, especially in the dwellings of the families of substance – perhaps because it allowed the householder to make a show of status and wealth in the closely packed ranks of costly oak studs paraded across the front of the home. Soon after the Middle Ages prosperous villagers in most parts of England showed a preference for close studding, though in the uplands and the west the studs did not always stand a full storey tall but were jointed into middle rails.

In the Midlands and the west the less wealthy and fashion-conscious home-makers continued to favour their local tradition of 'square panel' framing, with upright and horizontal timbers dividing the walls into panels of around a yard square. Those who wished to make rather more of a show would either prefer close studding or else opt for decorative framing, in which the square panels were subdivided by lesser timbers to create geometrical and ornamental displays. Examples of decorative framing are not particularly common and are mainly found in towns or isolated manor houses. Sometimes status was only proclaimed at ground-floor level, with the close-studded lower storey being surmounted by a storey of square panel work. There was also a great discrepancy in rural prosperity between the different ends of the country. Few modest cruck-framed houses were built in the south or Midlands of England after the Middle Ages, but in the northern villages a rather impoverished branch of the tradition survived well into the eighteenth century. In complete contrast, in the wealthy counties of Kent and Sussex scores of affluent villagers and farmers were occupying dwellings of real size and substance during the fifteenth

Buildings of local stone seem to grow organically out of the landscape. Right: thatched houses at Abbotsbury, Dorset. Below: Thwaite, near Hawes, where streambed, bridge and houses all blend with each other and with the stony setting. Opposite: stone and red pantiles in the largely eighteenth-century landscape of West Tanfield.

century. These were 'Wealden houses' in which a hall, open to the rafters, formed the central bay and was flanked on each side by two-storey bays, the whole being covered by a great hipped roof. More of these genuinely desirable houses were built as the style expanded into East Anglia and the Midlands in the sixteenth century.

Whatever type of framing was adopted, timber formed the structural skeleton of the house. The spaces between the timbers had to be filled to make a draughtproof home. Most popular were panels of wattle and daub, used from very early times until the eighteenth century. Upright staves of oak were slotted into the beams and then a basketwork of hazel or cleft oak wattles was woven between the staves. The wattle was then plastered in a daub of clay, chopped straw and dung, and when this was dry the panel was then limewashed or colourwashed. Where the studs were set too closely together to allow wattle panels to be woven, then horizontal laths were stacked up to fill the gaps and a similar daub was applied. Alternatively, an infill of stone rubble might be used, while from the sixteenth century onwards brickwork, sometimes built in herringbone patterns, was adopted as a higher status panel-filler. Some very fine timber-framed village houses were built during the seventeenth century, but in the eighteenth century the tradition declined and most of the later dwellings built in this way were cheap cottages for labourers and estate workers which economized on materials. The framing timbers used were thin and light and the panels were filled with a walling of 'clam-staff and daub' or 'mud and stud'. Upright staves were nailed to the frame and then plastered over with a very thick mud-based daub.

By Georgian times timber framing, even in its most expensive and showy forms, was considered distinctly unfashionable and many attempts were made to render over once distinguished exteriors or even to graft on fashionably symmetrical façades in brick and plasterwork. Meanwhile, the timber and daub panels of cottages of a poorer quality were concealed for reasons of protection as well as taste, particularly in the south. In East Anglia weatherboarding in horizontal planks of elm was popular, slates or clay tiles masked many a lightweight frame, while in Kent and Sussex mathematical tiles were introduced in the late eighteenth century. Though resembling the then fashionable bricks, these hung and interlocking tiles did not incur the Brick Taxes introduced in 1784.

As one would expect, stone-built villages are most common in settings which could offer a tolerably durable stone. Occasionally, however, stone cottages are found in geologically deprived areas with strong timber-framing traditions. The examples which spring most easily to mind are the flint dwellings of Norfolk and parts of the south coast. Flint occurs naturally within chalk strata but in Cambridgeshire chalk or 'clunch', normally considered too soft and porous except in shielded church interiors, was hewn into blocks and used for low-cost village housing. The division between the timber- and stone-building areas was not a timeless one and in the northern uplands the Great Rebuilding resulted in the gradual replacement of an old cruck-framing tradition with one which saw the dwellings of the poorer country folk translated into stone or else encased in it. Equally, in localities which had both woods and quarries, the building fashion could vary according to the relative costs of oak and rock, so that villages of mixed timber and stone dwellings would develop.

At the end of the Middle Ages England was still largely a country of timber buildings, with most of the exceptions being churches, castles and a few dwellings in places rich in stone. William Harrison observed that even the towns of the kingdom were built in timber, with a few exceptions – such as the stone dwellings in Welsh country towns. Yet in other places which were well endowed with stone, like Cornwall and the Yorkshire Dales, the timber and mud tradition still persisted – as it did even in the vicinity of many of the most renowned quarries. During the seventeenth and eighteenth centuries the rising aspirations of the villagers and local problems with timber supplies resulted in many village landscapes being translated from timber to stone. The dwellings were largely built by craftsmen. The purchaser or landlord would tell the local rough mason what was desired in terms of size, layout of rooms and cost. Given the perpetual difficulties with transport, the materials would either be hewn from the nearby quarry or gathered from the fields in the places where flint was used.

The dwellings could only be built from what was locally available. In a few places, like the Cotswolds or Northamptonshire uplands, villagers could exploit top-grade limestones and, occasionally, even have the stones sawn to present smooth ashlar faces. Usually, however, walls were of irregular rubble or of crudely squared and coursed material. Frequently the local rubble was fit for walling but for little else. This involved the home-makers in the unwelcome expense of importing a rather better grade of stone for the making of quoins, lintels and door and window dressings. Thatch remained the standard roofing material, except in some favoured localities where unusual types of stone could be quarried. True slates were largely confined to Cornwall and the Lake District, but, in parts of the limestone belt running from Northamptonshire to Dorset, there were some stones, sometimes known as 'potlids', which could be

*Mevagissey, in Cornwall,
was a planned fishing
village laid out about
1410 round a natural
harbour.*

split by the frost to yield thin roofing slabs. Meanwhile, sandstone
'thackstones' or thatching stones were quarried at various places in
the north and in the Charnwood Forest hamlets were roofed in the
rough but true Swithland slates.

The roofs of old village dwellings are always worth a second
glance. Roofs which are steeply pitched were almost always
originally thatched, while those clad in the local false slates had
shallow pitches to minimize the weight of the heavy burden to be
carried. Road improvements and rail transport allowed the great
commercial slate quarries developing in north Wales, Cornwall and
the Lake District to send their wares across village England. Pantiles
and other baked clay tiles were also dispersed, but not so widely. In
the old village many steep-roofed cottages which are now capped in
slate or tile were formerly clad in wheatstraw from fields nearby.
The gable wall may also have a tale to tell, for here one may detect a
faint line or break in walling showing how a wall was raised to add an
upper storey, or else see how the end walls were lengthened and the
roof lowered over them to form an 'outshut' extension.

Brick was late to make its debut on the village stage. Neglected
since Roman days, brick was used for domestic buildings in very few
medieval towns, like Hull, but became highly fashionable as a
material for prestigious mansions in Tudor and Elizabethan times.
Narrow, hand-made bricks first appeared in the homes of the more
ordinary country folk as a fire-proof means of building chimneys –
important status symbols in the Elizabethan village. Meanwhile,
brick nogging was also used as an expensive but decorative substitute

Cottages built for Georgian and Victorian farm workers. Above: brick construction at Avebury Trusloe, in Wiltshire.
Below: re-thatching work at Great Sampford, Essex.

for wattle and daub in the panels of timber-framed dwellings. Later it was a substitute for stone and formed the lintels and quoins of flint-walled houses. Though at first a luxury material, brick became the leading vernacular building material in the English Midlands and the Vale of York, its realm being divided by the great Dorset to Northamptonshire limestone belt, where stone maintained its sway. The early industries were localized and small in scale, with the first brick villages growing in places with good clays and the fuel supplies needed to fire the kilns. Differences in clay and technique resulted in numerous vernacular styles and contrasts, like the bright-red brickwork and pantiles of villages in the Newark area or the thick, burnt-chocolate bricks of the Trent valley villages. Brick and tile

making usually went together, but roofing tiles were often adopted to replace thatch in places like parts of Lincolnshire and the North York Moors where stone still reigned as a walling material.

Some places were bereft of building materials or the resources to buy them. Yet such localities could always turn to cob, with broad walls being built up in deep layers of compacted earth or clay, which could be seasoned and strengthened with some chalk if any was to hand. Limewash was needed to protect such walls. Some cob villages can still be enjoyed in Devon and Somerset, but the cob legacy in Wessex is much reduced and has virtually disappeared from the south of Leicestershire. Another resort of the impoverished home-maker was clay lump. While cob was built up in situ, clay lump consisted of a mixture of clay and straw shaped into large building blocks. These were laid on a plinth of tarred brick, bonded together with mud and then plastered to keep out the damp.

Mass production and mass transport spelled doom for the vernacular tradition in village architecture. Cheap imported softwoods brought commercial decline to the ancient oak woodlands. Slates produced in their millions at great quarry sites in the west offered roofs which would last a century but would not burn. Standardized bricks from the vast brickworks were more competitive than attractive – but they ousted the local products, closed many a quarry and made wattle and daub a thing of legend. There was no great shift in philosophy to ignite the change – villagers had always sought to build as much as they could for as little as possible. Factory, railway, canal and turnpike allowed them to build a little more for a little less, and it was only the village scenery that suffered.

Agricultural cottages at Winfrith, in Dorset, are of humbler materials: local earth and straw.

9 Special cases

We have explored the English village as the abode of a community permanently enmeshed in the task of survival. The great majority of English villages were indeed the dormitories of peasant labour forces, but there was always a minority of villages with other priorities. They included fishing settlements and places sustained by industry. In addition, a new group of villages emerged in the eighteenth and nineteenth centuries, born out of the whims, fancies and benevolence of their wealthy creators and sometimes labelled as 'villages of vision'. In reality the categories were not as exclusive as one might imagine. In medieval times there were many villages that housed some industrial workers alongside the larger land-working classes. In North Yorkshire, for example, some Nidderdale villages shared the spur-making industry of nearby Ripon and the linen manufacture of Knaresborough. At the same time, even the most substantial of the medieval towns housed considerable numbers of people who cultivated the town fields, while most village industrial workers were also smallholders of one kind or another.

Although they are now almost extinct, village fishing communities occupy a special niche in our imagination; the fortitude of the old fisherfolk and the disasters which they so frequently faced were real enough. There were fishermen in England for thousands of years before the dawn of farming, but because of the smallness of catches, the perishable nature of the product and, perhaps most importantly, the difficulties in distributing the catch, fishing remained a fairly small-scale and part-time activity for most of the Middle Ages. Most medieval fishermen were also feudal peasants who were bound to a coastal manor. W. G. Hoskins has described how an early fishing

Holmfirth near Huddersfield is an industrial village which erupted at the start of the nineteenth century.

community might have developed. East Somerton in Norfolk was a normal peasant village in Saxon times – except that in winter part of its population seems to have migrated to the coastal huts of a seasonal settlement at nearby Winterton. Here the peasants would sail their boats to exploit the run of codling, before returning to their fields in the spring. But by Norman times Winterton had become established as a village in its own right. Even the great port of Yarmouth seems to have begun in Saxon days as a seasonal hut settlement on a sandy island in the mouth of the Yare, a place which was occupied only when the herring shoaled in the autumn.

While part-time fishing for a very local market must have taken place along the coasts of England from very early times, few fishing villages are as old as their inland neighbours. For example, Sandsend, on the coastal strip of the North York Moors, started early and had a manorial sea fishery and some fifty-three cottages when the village was first recorded in 1254. Picturesque Staithes, later associated with the explorer Captain James Cook, was not mentioned until 1415, when it was a mere 'staithe' or landing-place serving the former village of Seaton. Robin Hood's Bay, appearing like an archetypal 'olde worlde' fishing village, does not seem to have existed before the sixteenth century. The story of Staithes and Winterton, which both grew as coastal satellites of more conventional villages, was repeated along the length of the English coastline and led to the creation of some of the most visited and renowned of our fishing settlements – like Looe and Mevagissey in Cornwall. Mevagissey seems to have been a planned village of around 1410. It was created around a triangular green facing the cliff-girt inlet selected as a harbour.

Cornwall is more closely associated with fishing villages than any other county, but here too the coastal settlements were later developments. The organization of the industry may have begun as a way of staving off the economic gloom which followed the disaster of the Black Death, and only Polperro and Port Isaac may have existed as villages previously. As the fishing settlements grew, so the harbour filled the central role played by the market green in inland villages. The fishermen built their homes beside the quay or around courtyards. The ground floors of these dwellings were open and existed as fish cellars where the catch was salted and packed in tubs. By the start of the seventeenth century the industry was beginning to specialize in pilchard fishing. Part-timers still had a prominent place, for the pilchard shoals entered Cornish waters after the harvest, when many farmers and landworkers switched to fishing.

Railway building extended the lives of many village fishing communities during the nineteenth century by allowing the swift

Portquin, in Cornwall, reputedly became a ghost town overnight when all its fishing fleet was sunk.

transport of fish to markets. But overfishing and the steady centralization of the industry in a few large ports with huge markets and bulk-handling facilities have spelled the end for fishing as a village industry. Not everybody mourned the passing of this perilous lifestyle. Cornish tradition holds that little Portquin became a ghost town overnight when a storm sank its entire fishing fleet and drowned all the men – though a more sober version tells that the port was deserted when it ceased to export antimony, an agent once used by dyers.

More often than not bustle and razzmatazz rather than gloom and decay are the hallmarks of the failed fishing village, for just as better facilities were sucking the industry into specialist ports, so the railways were bringing the seaside within reach of the masses. Fish cellars became shops and cafés; locals with salt on their whiskers forsook the perils of the reefs for a more certain income from ferrying anglers to and fro, while the empty berths in the harbour filled with pleasure craft. During the Middle Ages Cromer in Norfolk was a market town and port with a fleet which fished the Icelandic waters, but then decline set in and by the eighteenth century it was a mere fishing village. At the start of the next century it was discovered by tourists as an excellent resort for bathing and within a few decades it boasted four hotels, an inn and seventy boarding houses. In 1837 a sea storm swept the lot away, but the arrival of the railway in 1876 gave tourism a new lease of life and Cromer found a more sedate way to earn its living.

The glamour and picturesque attributes of the fishing village were not always shared by its inland industrial counterparts. In medieval times much, if not most, industry was based around the village, while the forges of the iron industry often burned in the depths of the greenwood and cloth fulling mills clattered beside lonely streams. There were specialized quarrying villages, like Barnack in Cambridgeshire, Ketton in Northamptonshire and Corfe in Dorset, and some villages which were deliberately founded to exploit a particular

The communal pump and courtyard at the purpose-built quarry village of Edmonton.

Corfe in Dorset, a medieval quarrying village.

resource. Greenhow Hill in North Yorkshire is said to be the most lofty village in England. It was created in 1613 to allow a community of lead miners to live close to their work. The surrounding moor was enclosed to support the oxen and horses used in the mines and the miners were provided with smallholdings. The Industrial Revolution produced its equivalent of the medieval stone-hewing villages in settlements built to house quarry-workers, such as Egypt and Thornton Heights near Bradford. A more quaint example is Edmonton in Cornwall, built for twenty-four families of quarry-workers at the Camel Quarry. The terraced cottages were positioned flanking a rectangular courtyard which had the village pump at its centre; a chapel and the court house where the manager lived and had his office faced each other across the yard.

In most cases, however, the growth of industrial villages was a slow and haphazard process. As the Yorkshire textile industry grew in the seventeenth and eighteenth centuries, countless villagers and farmers became involved in home-based spinning and weaving. Frequently, impoverished weavers would set up home above the fields of an established village, enclosing some land from the edge of the moor for pasture. In the humble homestead on the moorland edge the man would weave, while his wife would spin yarn and tend the stock on the little holding. Such settlements multiplied in the countryside surrounding the great magnets provided by wool markets such as Halifax. The markets imported and exported wool, which came back to market and then back again in the forms of yarn, woven cloth, and fulled and finished cloth.

The rural industrial workers spent much time travelling back and forth on market roads with their pack ponies. But in some places hamlets or villages of cloth workers grew up, with neighbours engaging in different stages of manufacture and passing their products on from house to house, so reducing the time spent in journeying to market. In due course, warehouses, workshops and mills were established at these nuclei to bring a new industrial settlement into being. In other places weavers' cottages were slotted into the gaps between the farmsteads of existing agricultural villages, such as Heptonstall, Slaithwaite or Linthwaite. Sometimes the rise of factory-based industry centred on huge urban mills engulfed the formerly freestanding villages in a sea of terraced housing – so that all that survived of the village was the name of an industrial suburb. Bradford, Huddersfield and Manchester are great agglomerations of absorbed industrial and agricultural villages.

The growth of industrial villages could be rapid and chaotic – Holmfirth in Yorkshire was a case in point. Until 1784 the bottom of the valley, which had formed part of a lonely medieval hunting chase, had a manorial corn mill, old fulling mills and a few cottages. Then a wool clothier established a mill and by 1822 Holmfirth was described in a directory as follows:

The houses are scattered in the deep valley, and on the acclivities of the hills, without regard to arrangement, or the formation of streets . . . The traveller, at his first view of this extraordinary village, is struck with astonishment at the singularity of its situation and appearance . . . This is a place of great trade, and the principal part of the inhabitants are employed in the manufacture of woollen cloth.

As the blackening terraces advanced, manufacturing was sucked out of the freestanding cottages and villages, away from hand or water-powered workshops and into the great coal-fuelled factories of the industrial boom towns. Very frequently the workers were sucked in too, so that memories of village life and of the long treks on market lanes vanished behind a pall of smoke and the clatter of regiments of shuttles. The landscape of squatters' cottages, hamlets and villages created by the Yorkshire textile industry was duplicated in other industrial areas. In the Black Country, for example, settlements rose and fell around the homes and workshops of their squatter founders. Mushroom Green has a name which suggests it sprang up overnight. Before its decline it existed as a scatter of red-brick dwellings which were occupied by nailmakers.

In the case of the lead industry of the Pennines, it was foreign competition which brought this rural activity to its downfall. It had probably existed since prehistoric times, and on the eve of the Industrial Revolution Derbyshire villagers could stake their claims to thirty yards (twenty-seven metres) of ground by taking a dish of good sample ore to the Barmaster. They divided their time equally between their mines and the land, working about six hours per day on each. Above villages like Bonsall one can still see the filled-in shafts and the tumbling walls of the huts or 'coes' where the part-time miners changed clothes and kept their tools. As investment and technology changed the industry, some of them migrated to nearby mill towns. At first the cotton mill owners built high-quality housing to attract their workers. Arkwright's Cromford, which expanded from a tiny existing village nucleus, is a good example.

Further north, in Swaledale, most lead miners had become full-time employees by the nineteenth century. During the last quarter of that century the industry decayed and parishes which had become almost urban in character lost up to three-quarters of their population and became rural once again. Gunnerside village is something of a backwater today but it has a Methodist church, which held a congregation of 500, and two junior schools, which each accommodated 90 children. But most of the villagers disappeared a century ago in search of work in the mills of Lancashire, leaving the chimneys, smelters and wheels to decay. While the lead mines were flourishing in Swaledale, just over the watershed in Wensleydale there were villages like Gayle which were partly peopled by hand-knitters. And over the next watershed in Nidderdale, linen, rope making, cotton and lead smelting created a chain of industrial villages and hamlets.

Industrial villages were less resilient than their agricultural neighbours. The more finite the resource and the more specialized the skill, the frailer the dependent communities tended to be. Coal mining produced the broadest shoulders, the bravest hearts and the weakest villages, particularly in the north-east of England. As collieries closed, communities of miners were left stranded and jobless. In 1954 the County Durham planners introduced a 'category D' classification for industrial villages which would no longer be sustained by local government funds. With all life-support systems switched off, it was hoped that the afflicted communities would disperse to find employment in new and expanded towns. Some death-row villages attracted commuters and earned a reprieve, while others were bulldozed before their crumbling ruins could harbour drifters and vandals. Hedley Hill, East Howle, Page Bank and several others lie in the graveyard of village England. Today the threat of decay lurks wherever colliery villages remain. Creswell in Derbyshire was built for Emerson Bainbridge MP at the end of the nineteenth century, when 250 dwellings were created for the mining families. Now its day as a colliery village has been declared over and the remains of many a lost miner may rest in the silence of the forgotten galleries.

During the Middle Ages various villages were evicted from the precincts of monasteries, the confines of hunting parks and other suddenly unwelcoming places. Sometimes humanity – or, just as likely, the practicalities of estate management – resulted in the creation of a replacement village for the dispossessed. Nobody at this time regarded the English village with sentiment, any more than we would see Soweto or the shanty suburbs of Brazil as places of romance. Attitudes tinged with whimsy arose much later, but as landscaped parks were created, titivated and expanded in Georgian times, and as the communities of old villages were ejected from these contrived and sanitized settings, then ideas began to change. It occurred to some landlords and their architects that, were a new settlement to be provided, it might not be just a ramshackle and functional place like the old village. Perhaps it could be a vehicle for expressing new notions of rustic romance? Perhaps it could contain all those quaint frills and embellishments so much part of the romantic idyll but sadly lacking in the real village?

The motives of those who created new villages of vision are open to question. In the case of some industrialists, a genuinely benevolent paternalism fuelled the desire to build more humane settings for manufacturing life. In many of the new estate villages too the conditions of daily life were raised considerably. The rural landlords, however, do not seem to have consulted their tenants about the practical necessities of home life. They often seem to have been more concerned about the aesthetic effect that the pretty new cottages would have upon important guests as they approached the gates of their park.

The extremes of rustic myth-making were achieved in the mid-nineteenth century by Lord Ongley at Old Warden in Bedfordshire. Not only did he provide thatched cottages festooned with barge boards, lattices, curving dormers and a wealth of other extravagant details but he also added a cast of actors. Villagers were obliged to inhabit this stage set of rural whimsy wearing tall hats and red cloaks in order to complement the artificial world of grouped shrubs and honey-tinted houses.

The inspiration for the quaintly bizarre cottages ornées at Old Warden and a score of other such villages derived largely from Blaise Hamlet, built near Bristol in 1810. Nostalgia for the mythical rural world – and cottage designs to evoke it – already existed, but the Quaker banker, John Scandrett Harford, produced a whole village of Picturesque dwellings and inserted a population of impoverished elderly retainers to add to the sentiment. John Nash and George Repton designed the nine tiny cottages which were grouped around their 'village green', each one unique and irregular, just as the script dictated, and with much care being given to the parodying of Elizabethan chimney designs. Once installed, the worthy poor may well have liked their new homes, though in no time at all this monument to Picturesque ideals became the destination of excursions from Clifton and Bristol.

Soon new and replacement model villages were erupting throughout the British Isles. Somerleyton in Suffolk, dating from 1850, was inspired by Blaise, so that each dwelling was different from its neighbour. Picturesque timber framing was favoured at Victorian Acton Burnell in Shropshire; at the rebuilt villages of Ripley and

Blaise Hamlet, near Bristol, is an artificial village designed by John Nash, evoking a rural past that was almost entirely mythical.

New Wimpole in Cambridgeshire Tudor themes were evoked in stone and brick respectively, while at Belton in Lincolnshire both Tudor and Jacobean designs were featured. There were some purpose-built villages which predated Blaise. Harewood near Harrogate succeeded several emparked villages and was built outside the park gates for Edwin Lascelles by Carr of York. The architecture was not Picturesque, but rather formal and severe. Gritstone terraces housed estate workers, with the grander officials enjoying more spacious accommodation, while a ribbon factory was included in an attempt to diversify employment. In Oxfordshire the original estate village at Great Tew is thought to have dated back to the mid-seventeenth century, while in the same county Nuneham Courtenay, which provided Goldsmith with his inspiration, replaced nearby Newnham early in the 1760s.

Amongst the most distinctive of the early model villages are the seven Moravian settlements established in England and Ireland in the forty years following 1744. The Moravians were a socialistic German Protestant sect who modelled their villages on their native prototype of Herrnhut. Residents engaged in various trades, but donated their profits to the community, receiving wages in return. Later villages, like Fairfield near Manchester, were built to square layouts with gardens, elegant chapels, schools and a range of public facilities. The original English Moravian settlement, Fulneck near Pudsey, was established on a particularly difficult hillside site and had to be built

Terraces of mock-Tudor cottages resulted from the rebuilding of Ripley in the first half of the nineteenth century.

at great cost with parallel terraces at different levels. Even so, the Classical architecture of the school and chapel are of a high quality. No less worthy of a visit is Abbeydale Hamlet, now engulfed by the spread of Sheffield. Under the patronage of Earl Fitzwilliam a trio of cottages were established in 1789 to house workers who forged and ground the hand tools used at the riverside ironworks. A house for the manager was built here in the 1830s, but a century later the hamlet became deserted. During the 1960s the lost industrial world was re-created and Abbeydale has become a magnet for visitors.

Of the model industrial villages, Saltaire, near Keighley, is the earliest and perhaps the most interesting. The grand patron was Sir Titus Salt, who had introduced alpaca wool in the manufacture of worsted. He sought to establish a new industrial community beside the Aire on the more verdant fringes of the Bradford mill conurbation. During the 1850s and '60s more than 500 terraced dwellings were built, with the Italianate architecture chosen finding its most pleasing expression in the great Renaissance palace of the mill and the imposing non-Conformist church. Lighter Italianate touches appeared on the terraces and almshouses. The Institute was more flamboyant, while a laundry and a library were provided to serve the whole community in their different ways. The Saltaire vision may have derived from model villages described in Disraeli's novels *Coningsby* and *Sybil*. The village certainly offered a more uplifting setting for life than that experienced by the vast majority of industrial workers. The rectangular grid layout, the public facilities, the green flanked by almshouses and the views on open countryside – all contrasted with the grey jumbled terraces of the working world stretched out to the south. Saltaire succeeded and grew, and, though now threatened by road-building plans, it is, in its way, as fascinating as any 'olde worlde' Domesday village.

As Salt was creating Saltaire, other model villages were forming nearby; Copley and Akroydon near Halifax were created by the politician and mill owner, Edward Akroyd, MP, while Crossleys, the carpet barons, also built their West Hill Park estate at Halifax. In the decades that followed, model industrial suburbs and villages became almost commonplace. Bournville in Warwickshire arose in the 1890s as the first industrial garden village and was built for the Cadbury workers. The rival chocolate makers, Rowntrees, situated their model factory village of New Earswick near York at the start of the twentieth century. Barlaston in Staffordshire was put up in 1936 to succeed the old Wedgwood factory and village at Etruria; Silver End in Essex was built for the Crittall employees in the 1920s and Stewartby in Bedfordshire was established at the same time to house workers for the London Brick Company. Then there are the new villages created on green-field sites to accommodate commuter populations. These, of course, are the developer's dream and the

The industrialist Titus Salt built the model village of Saltaire, near Bingley, for his own workers, providing nearly every amenity to keep them healthy and contented. Below: the factory where most of them worked.

The almshouse and Reformed church at Saltaire. The whole little town was built to a consistently high architectural standard that still commands admiration.

conservationist's nightmare. New Ash Green in Kent, begun in 1965, and Bar Hill Village in Cambridgeshire, of a similar vintage, are examples.

Finally, there are those bizarre rural settlements, the rows of squatter shanties found in the rural fringes of the Black Country. The shanties developed in the years following the First World War, when urban workers persuaded local farmers to lease them lands for home and holiday use. Most of the dwellings were homemade from odds and ends of cheap materials, expanded in haphazard manners, embellished with whatever fanciful frills and motifs tickled their makers' fancy and painted from a rainbow palette. Even so, they have survived the onslaught of later planning legislation and many shanties have been inherited by successive generations. Shanties erupted here and there, singly, in pairs or in clusters, but sometimes weaving and swaying in wandering lines where farmers have parted with fringes of land along the boundaries of adjacent fields. The shanty settlements are the antithesis of the stereotyped attempts to create synthetic villages at places like Bar Hill, and, to many less inhibited thinkers, rather more appealing.

10 The village on its knees

'Enclosure' is a dry and dusty word; it does not fire the imagination like 'Conquest', 'Reformation', 'Harrying' or 'Anarchy'. And yet it played a far greater part in the transformation of rural England than all these other traumas put together. Striking over several lifetimes, it eventually killed old village England stone dead. It was a campaign of privatization, one which converted the village strip fields, shared meadows and commons into parcels of private property, and it proceeded piecemeal, each parish having its own particular Act of enclosure. In 1604 the first Act privatized the commons at Radipole in Dorset, though hardly anybody imagined that this backwater event heralded the greatest rural revolution since the adoption of open field farming. More than a century passed before the campaign gained much momentum, but between about 1750 and 1850 village life was transformed. When the last Act was passed in 1914, enclosure had affected about 5400 parishes and 7 million acres (2.8 million hectares) of rural England.

To set the changes in motion, the leading lights in a particular parish would petition Parliament for an Act of enclosure – and Parliament would almost invariably oblige. Then commissioners were appointed to oversee the changes, men of substance in the community who were generally chosen by the powerful local promoters of enclosure, and they would employ a surveyor and a valuer. The object of the exercise was to disentangle the age-old pattern of intermeshed strips and shared commons and reallocate land in the form of compact private blocks. The holding that a family received at the end of the day was intended to be equivalent to their rights in the shared resources before enclosure. But the whole effect

The typical English landscape after the Enclosure Acts – a patchwork of compact, private fields divided by hedges: Lower Langford, Avon, taken from Dolebury Warren hillfort.

Opposite: Polperro, one of the few Cornish fishing villages that existed before the Black Death of 1348.

was to make the rich richer and the village poor destitute to the point of migration.

The controversy engaged some of the brightest minds in England and opinion was fiercely divided. Thomas Tusser, an Essex man, was an early champion of good husbandry who died twenty-four years before the first Act of enclosure. However, he was able to make a contrast between farming in regions without open fields and farming where open fields still held sway. He wrote:

> The Country enclosed I praise,
>   The t'other delighteth not me!
> For nothing the wealth it doth raise,
>   To such as inferior be,
> How both of them partly I know,
> Here somewhat I mind to show.

He went on to enthuse about the advantages of enclosure and the destruction wrought in the contrasting, open countryside:

> More plenty of Mutton and Beef,
>   Corn, butter, and cheese of the best,
> More wealth anywhere (to be brief),
>   More people, more handsome and prest,
> Where find ye? Go search any coast,
> Than where inclosure is most.

Others would take a different view. The Northamptonshire poet John Clare lived through the heyday of enclosure and complained passionately about its effect on English life and landscape. In his 'Lubin's Anguish' of 1821 he wrote:

> There once were lanes in nature's freedom dropt,
> There once were paths that every valley wound,
> Inclosure came and every path was stopt;
> Each tyrant fix'd his sign where paths were found,
> To hint a trespass now who cross'd the ground:
> Justice is made to speak as they command;
> The high road now must be each stint'd bound:
> – Inclosure, thou'rt curse upon the land,
> And tasteless was the wretch who thy existence plann'd.

The beneficiaries of enclosure were the rich landowners and the tenants of substance, but at the intellectual level the argument raged between humanitarian ideals and sentimentalists, like John Clare, Oliver Goldsmith or William Cobbett, on the one side and the advocates of efficiency as the key to prosperity, like Arthur Young, on the other. Yet even Young recognized that the village poor were being assailed in a way they could not resist. He decided that 'by nineteen out of twenty Enclosure Acts the poor was injured, and most grossly' – although this was, he believed, partly the result of the knavery of commissioners and attorneys. He quoted one commissioner who admitted that his work had injured 2000 poor people at the rate of twenty families per parish, and he added: 'The poor in these parishes may say, and with truth, "Parliament may be tender of property: all I know is that I had a cow and an Act of Parliament has taken it from me".'

Enclosure persecuted the parish poor in several ways. Those, many of them squatters, who existed solely on the varied resources of the common and had no title or tenancy won nothing from enclosure. When the common was gone, then so were they. Others, who had rights to the common and only a humble share in the village pool of land, emerged as smallholders – but then they had to bear the cost of hedging or walling a plot which could not compare in value with the rights they had lost. Soon such people would sell up and go, perhaps emigrating or treading the road to the urban factories – those very factories that had extinguished rural crafts. While the poor struggled and failed to meet the obligatory costs of fencing, the lords of manors were awarded an extra sixteenth of the land in lieu of their surface rights. The cottager, meanwhile, became a landless labourer. At the same time all the village officials who had supervised the smooth operation of the old arrangements lost their jobs. Nobody would now employ a pinder, a hayward, a village cowherd, a shepherd or a peeper to warn of dangerous chimneys.

Enclosure and other ills brought chaos to the village community. In his *Rural Rides*, published in 1830, Cobbett wrote: 'In all the really agricultural villages and parts of the kingdom, there is shocking decay; a great dilapidation and constant pulling down or falling down of houses. The farm-houses are not so many as they were by three fourths.' In fact, enclosure caused huge gaps to appear in the village landscape. In medieval times most of the dwellings were, in a sense, farm houses, for their occupants farmed shares in the common fields. By the Victorian age farm houses made up only a small part of the village housing stock and families which had done well from enclosure often chose to quit the old village homestead and build a new one on the land block which enclosure had provided for them. Many of England's solitary farmsteads date from Georgian and early-Victorian times and stand as memorials to farming families who rose in the world and left the close village community for the convenience of 'living on the job'.

We have heard the conflicting voices of the cognoscenti, like Clare, Cobbett and Young, but what about those of the people who

*Gayle, in Wensleydale,
was renowned as a
village of hand-knitters
in the eighteenth century.*

*Right: estate housing at
Holkham, Norfolk,
where the original village
was shifted and grafted
onto an existing hamlet
in the 1760s, and where a
Tudor-style village was
subsequently built at the
gates of the aristocratic
park.*

bore the brunt of the changes? The most quoted and quotable snippet of opinion was offered by Arthur Young in the *Annals of Agriculture*: 'Go to an ale-house kitchen of an old enclosed country, and there you will see the origin of poverty and poor-rates. For whom are they to be sober? For whom are they to save? For the parish? If I am diligent, shall I have leave to build a cottage? If I am sober, shall I have land for a cow? If I am frugal, shall I have half an acre of potatoes? You offer no motives; you have nothing but a parish officer and a workhouse! – Bring me another pot –.'

This cry from the heart encapsulates the plight of the villager broken by enclosure. Overnight he had become less than his villein ancestors of five centuries earlier. The villeins were part of the village with useful tasks to perform, a word in the village council and with rights in the landstock of the community. They were of the blood of the village, and that counted. But the hopeless cottager and land-starved tenant were outcasts who no longer had a role in the community or a legal claim to remain in the village. Their misery and humiliation were complete – for what is a peasant without land? Why not drink away the meagre proceeds of dispossession and spit upon the future? Arthur Young was told how enclosure had affected the small-fry of St Neots: '. . . the poor were ill-treated by having about half a rood given to them in lieu of a cow keep, the inclosure of which land costing more than they could afford, they sold the lots at £5, the money was drank out at the ale-house and the men, spoiled by habit, came, with their families, to the parish.'

The victims of enclosure either became landless labourers or else lie buried in the public graveyards of manufacturing towns or mouldering in far-flung former colonies. Though many of them were alive but a century ago, they are now gone and forgotten. Knock on village doors today and ask the occupants what Parliamentary Enclosure was all about and nobody but perhaps a stray historian or the brightest pupil will know.

Enclosure swept away the commoners and smallholders but the fields of England were still crowded with labourers at haytime and harvest. The booming cry of the corncrake still found a counterpoint in the swishing of scythes and the rasp of corn stems against the sickle. Children were still needed to frighten the rooks at seedtime; horse and ox still planted their hoofs in the ploughsoil and hauled their loads as they had done for thousands of years. Once peopled by peasants of every kind, the crowded fields were not populated by farmers and their hirelings – but the need for hedgers and ditchers, ploughmen, stockmen and carters, hands to cast the seed corn, hands

The days of the crowded fields are evoked in this late-Victorian scene depicting threshing and stacking. At haytime the whole labour resource of the village was mobilized, women and children as well as men.

to pick stones from the cold earth and hands to steer the plough still remained.

The men who toiled in the fields now worked for a master and depended upon wages and the poor rate for survival. Many of them had been paid for their work before enclosure, but then they also had the freedom to gather their fuel and bedding on the common and to run a couple of milk cows, a nag or a few sheep with the village stock; some also had smallholdings. Though there was much to do, there were still too many workers. For the village labourer 'progress' meant starvation wages and a losing battle against the mechanization of the work which had always been done with hands, hoes and scythes. In 1811, when the first protests against mechanization were heard, agriculture was by far England's largest industry and some 6,129,000 people were dependent on farming and mining. In 1851 2,000,000 people were employed by farming; by 1871 the figure had fallen to 1,500,000 and by the end of the century more than 300,000 workers had fled the land.

During the greater part of the Middle Ages the most numerous type of villager was a villein. After enclosure the landless labourer took his place. According to a system devised by the magistrates of Berkshire while meeting at Speenhamland, near Newbury, in 1795, the villager's wages were supplemented by public funds to reach a level which was tied to the price of bread. In fact, he received less than the starvation level from the farmer, who was pleased to pay as little from his own pocket as he possibly could. The system survived until 1834, when the land worker was faced with the choices of

Overleaf:
The village in its fields. This is the view towards West Burton, in Wensleydale.

The end of a haymaking day near Swanley, Kent, about 1910. Note the cart with at least twenty-four children in it.

earning a living wage, dying of starvation or entering the humiliating world of the workhouse. Enclosure had robbed the village peasant of his pride, his independence and his security.

During the Napoleonic wars, when cheaper produce could not be imported, the prices of farm goods rocketed. The villagers saw their farmer masters taking on the airs and graces of squires, though the actual labourers did not share in the spoils. Later, however, they did share in the post-war collapse and by 1816 their bitterness and desperation erupted into revolt. In East Anglia the malcontents gathered at dusk; in grimy cottages gnarled hands scrawled out threatening letters, while in the distance the dark skies were lit by the flames from blazing ricks. In Suffolk a force of 1500 rioters formed and dispersed in bands. They demanded a cut in the price of bread and meat. They carried flags marked 'Bread or Blood' and bore staffs which were spiked and studded in iron. In Brandon the house of a loathed butcher called Willet was burned to the ground and the sheriff of the county sped to the Home Secretary to demand the despatch of troops.

Dragoons and yeomanry put down the unrest, but the Fen country had a stronger tradition of intransigence. At Littleport a mob of landworkers who had rioted in Ely were engaged in a battle, two of their number being killed and seventy-five taken prisoner. A Special Commission was convened to try the case. Five of the men were hanged and nine transported, five of them for life. One of the judges

A cartload of faggots in the Cotswolds, photographed before the 1914–18 War.

declared that the men were well paid and that any reduction in food prices would only result in more income being spent on drink.

The passage of time did not seem to brighten the lot of the village labourer and neither did it foster more merciful attitudes amongst the men of power. In 1830 starvation conditions again prevailed in the southern counties and many villagers looked to trade unionism as a means of raising their wages. In the Dorset village of Tolpuddle a local branch of the Friendly Society of Agricultural Labourers was formed by the impoverished farmhands, much to the distress of the landowners of the county. As trade unions were no longer illegal, the authorities persecuted the men under an archaic and irrelevant piece of legislation, the Unlawful Oaths Act of 1797, which was introduced at the time of the French Wars. It was claimed that the men had been involved in a strange initiation ceremony on joining the union. The fact that one of the leaders, George Lovelace, was a Methodist lay preacher of excellent character had no effect when the six men were sentenced at Dorchester in 1834. A great wave of indignation swept across the nation as the news spread that the men, now known as the Tolpuddle Martyrs, had been transported for seven years. All but a year of the sentences were served before the Martyrs received remission and returned to England.

The Tolpuddle Martyrs were not an isolated group of dissidents and victims. In the demonstrations of 1830-31 against starvation wages and the threshing machines which were thought to cause them,

Overleaf:
The angular geometry of Parliamentary enclosure fields around Darley, in Nidderdale; and the former market town of Askrigg, in Wensleydale, where the field walls, roofs and dwellings all express the necessity to use local building materials. The scene may be familiar to viewers of the James Herriott television series.

25 GUINEAS REWARD.

Henfield Prosecuting Society.

WHEREAS some evil disposed Person or Persons, did, in the Night of Tuesday, the 8th Instant, break open the Stable on Furzefield Farm, in the Parish of Shermanbury, in the occupation of Mr. THOMAS PAGE, and maliciously CUT OFF and carry away

THE HAIR

FROM THE

TAILS OF 3 CART HORSES

the property of the said THOMAS PAGE.

A REWARD OF

FIVE GUINEAS

will be given to any Person or Persons giving Information of the Offender or Offenders, so that he or they may be Convicted thereof; such Reward to be paid by the Treasurer of the said Society, immediately after such Conviction.

THOMAS COPPARD, Clerk.

HORSHAM, 9th MAY, 1838.

A FURTHER REWARD OF

20 GUINEAS

will be paid on such Conviction as aforesaid, by me

THOMAS PAGE.

Printed by Charles Hunt, West Street, Horsham.

The 1830s were years of unrest in the countryside. The formation of 'Prosecuting Societies' was only one symptom of the times.

Previous page: The transformation of the back yard, Bibury, Gloucestershire. We should not forget that however seductive these spaces are today, the half-starved villager of the past was more interested in keeping a pig than in growing a flower garden. Relics from the past are often gathered together to prettify a cottage garden and beside the cottage we can see a mushroom-shaped staddle-stone of the kind formerly used to support granaries above the reach of vermin.

three men were sent to the gallows and 420 transported to the penal settlements in Australia. Threshing provided the labourer with invaluable work during late autumn, winter and early spring when the farms lay semi-dormant. Every time that they saw a new threshing machine arriving at a farm the workers knew that the weeks ahead offered nothing but the pittance of parish relief. In their desperation they turned to rick-burning and to a mythical hero, Captain Swing. Like a latterday Robin Hood, Swing would ride across the countryside in a trail of fire, never stopping until the farmers abandoned their loathsome machines and enticed the workers back with living wages.

There is nothing to suggest that Swing ever really existed. The threatening letters that 'he' sent were penned by many other hands. Even so, his supporters exposed the weaknesses in the rule of the country establishments, for there were too few soldiers to enforce the rule of law upon the outraged rural masses. Troops apprehended a mob of 400 dissidents near Maidstone, though within a month much of Kent and Sussex was controlled by rioters and three regiments of dragoons were despatched. Then the revolt spread to Hampshire, where 1500 men smashed threshing machines and demanded 'contributions' from the houses of the wealthy. Here the labourers found a real 'Captain', a 'Captain Hunt', really a farm labourer and former soldier called Cooper. At Fordingbridge a threshing machine workshop was burned; at Selborne and Headley the workhouses were razed to the ground and the vicar of Selborne was forced to sign a paper pledging to reduce his tithes. Buckinghamshire, Berkshire, Dorset and Gloucestershire were all drawn into the uprising, which has become known as the Last Labourers' Revolt.

Like the peasants' revolts before, the Last Labourers' Revolt was ended by repression, and when Thomas Hood wrote his 'Lay of the Labourer' early in the 1840s the average farm wage in the southern counties of England was only 8s. 5d. (42p) per week. His verses accurately expressed the sentiments of those who had rebelled just a few years earlier:

> To a flaming barn or farm
>   My fancies never roam
> The fire I yearn to kindle and burn
>   Is on the hearth of Home;
> Where children huddle and crouch
>   Through dark long winter days,
> Where starving children huddle and crouch,
>   To see the cheerful rays,
> A-glowing on the haggard cheek,
>   And not in the haggard's blaze!
> Ay, only give me work,
>   And then you need not fear
> That I shall snare his worship's hare,
>   Or kill his grace's deer;
> Break into his lordship's house,
>   To steal the plate so rich;
> Or leave the yeoman that had purse
>   To welter in a ditch.

The village riots of the 1830s were partly sparked by the introduction of threshing machines, but mechanization had already undermined the independence of the cottager. At the end of the eighteenth century the age-old craft of spinning was gravitating into new factories. This change removed a vital source of cottage income and another of those options which had helped to diversify the village economy – for up to eight hand spinners had been needed to supply the yarn for each weaver in the days of the spinning wheel. Then, between about 1815 and 1830, the power looms of the factory began to take work away from thousands of villagers who had scraped together a living from a combination of farming and weaving. Many then faced no choice but to follow their work.

The Victorian era saw a great emptying of the crowded fields. The threshing devices had caused the greatest unrest, but soon machines

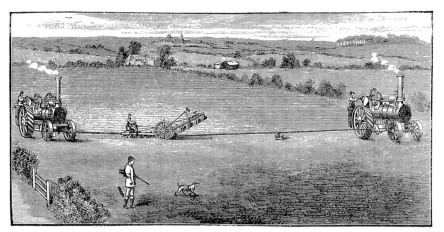

Two illustrations from a book published in 1889 showing the agricultural use of the steam engine. Above: double steam-ploughing, the plough being pulled to and fro across the field by engines placed on each side. Right: Proctor's Digger, for breaking up the soil.

were advancing on almost every task and routine around the farm. All-iron ploughs appeared at the start of the nineteenth century, though their arrival caused no real concern in the village. In the 1840s steam engines entered the farm, offering an awe-inspiring alternative to the power which had been provided by bone and sinew. In the 1850s engines with high-pressure boilers were introduced, with greatly improved power-to-weight ratios which made it much easier to reach the far-flung corners of the farm. The engines could be applied to the great tasks of the farming calendar, ploughing and threshing. A six-furrow plough hauled back and forth across the field between two engines could plough fourteen acres in a single

Opposite: two Yorkshire villages where identity has been almost submerged by summer visitors to the Dales: Reeth, near Richmond, once a centre of the lead industry, and Malham, a market for black cattle driven from Scotland.

day. Hitherto a ploughman and a pair of shire horses would take the same time to plough a single acre. The engines and accessories – cultivators, harrows and drain-diggers – cost some £1800, so that only the big farmers, who were also the big employers, could afford them. All available hands were still conscripted to the harvest fields, but in the latter part of the nineteenth century engineers strove to mechanize this last bastion of village employment. The breakthrough came in the 1880s with the introduction of binders, which not only cut the crop but also bound the sheaves ready for stacking.

Whatever the wrongs of the feudal system, lords did not normally fire their vassals and then evict them from their cottages. The community of the Victorian village was polarized in a different way. The lord had become a squire and the old feudal empire was now generally shared between him and a handful of large freehold and tenant farmers. They were the masters of the parish, controlling employment and also the tied homes of many of their labourers. On the whole they were deeply disliked and very few earned more than a grudging respect from the workforce. They had succeeded where the other sons of villeins had failed – and an important ingredient in many a success story was their willingness to be much more ruthless than their neighbours. In certain respects this harshness could almost be justified. The old tenants and smallholders had worked to subsist; any farm surplus which went to market was an added bonus. Victorian farming was much more commercial and therefore competitive. The farmer could argue that kindness and concern for his workforce marked the first step on the road to bankruptcy.

The real old village was not peopled by farmers. On the whole they lived outside the village; they distanced themselves from a community of villagers which feared and disliked them, and they generally sought to support a stable of hunters, a keeper or two and rise as far above the social world of the rural poor as they possibly could. The archetypal farmer, who was both the pillar and the scourge of the village community, was satirized by John Clare in his poem 'Farmer Finch':

> A Sunday never comes, or foul or fair,
> That misses him at church throughout the year.
> The priest himself boasts as the man's reward
> That he ne'er preached a sermon but he heard.
> Such is the man in public; all agree
> That saints themselves no better man could be.
> But now of private life let's take the view:
> In that same church and in that very pew

> Where he each Sabbath sings and reads and prays,
> He joins the vestry upon common days,
> Cheating the poor with levies double laid
> On their small means, that wealth may be defrayed:
> To save his own and others', his compeers,
> He robs the poor whom he has robbed for years,
> Making the house of prayer the house of sin
> And placing Satan as high priest within.

In Victorian times society was much more diverse than before. True, enclosure had made the various public officials who oversaw communal farming redundant – but many other types of villagers emerged to take their places. Cash and commerce overturned the old world of subsistence and self-sufficiency. The village became less of an agricultural dormitory and more of a service centre.

In the feudal village there were few specialists – only a miller and perhaps a blacksmith. The other crafts were performed by villeins on a part-time basis. In the Victorian age society was more mobile and more commercial. Transport conditions had been greatly improved by the turnpiking of roads. Any village of note had at least one firm of blacksmiths. As the rich became richer and mobility was increased, the demand for farriers for heavy horses, carriage horses, hacks and hunters steadily grew. More farm produce had to be shifted to depots and to the growing urban markets, so that there was plenty of work for the new village specialists like wheelwrights and cartwrights. The village economy was now a cash economy; whenever they could afford to, the locals paid for their coats and boots and shoes. In many cases the highlight of the farmworker's year was the Christmas trip to the shoemaker to purchase a new pair of work boots. The days of the commoner and the cottage smallholder were done. Food was a commodity to be bought from the local butcher and dairy; it could no longer be homegrown. The high-street shop, often lacking in the feudal village, gained precedence over the shabby stalls of the weekly market. People no longer lived in homemade shanties of mud, straw and sticks, so the village community often included a mason, brick-maker, joiner, slater or thatcher. In 1840 the penny post was introduced and soon the post office claimed its place on the village high street.

In due course the growing mobility that had helped to nurture the village specialists proved to be their undoing as village shoppers opted for the keener prices and wider ranges of products available in the towns. The Victorian village crafts, like milling, smithing, shoemaking, wheelwrighting and so on, were refinements of ancient traditional skills which had been honed and perfected over generations of craftsmanship. Gradually milling became concentrated in larger, more modern plants, shoes and clothes were mass-produced in factories, and machine-making enterprises, like Howard of Bedford or Fowlers of Leeds, took over the task of furnishing the farm. Some smiths and cartwrights survived for long enough to convert their workshops into garages for the motor age. But so many village enterprises have disappeared that it is now hard for us to imagine just how many different trades once flourished.

In 1851 the community of Masham in North Yorkshire included, amongst other tradespeople, 51 farm labourers, 17 dressmakers, 3 straw bonnet makers, 11 blacksmiths, 15 shoemakers and 58 house servants. Masham was relatively large, but at this time any village worth its salt supported at least one tailor, a cobbler (if not a shoemaker), a grocer, a butcher, several inns, a joiner and a blacksmith. In 1888 county councils were created, with rural districts and parish councils following in 1894. New officials were appointed, new tasks had to be performed and old ones improved, and so local functionaries and workers, such as teachers and roadmen, claimed a place in the community. Village society was still changing and in some places even the farmworkers became a minority in settlements which had hitherto existed because of their earth and pasture.

Meanwhile, the lot of the farm labourer worsened. During the last quarter of the nineteenth century English farming experienced depression. Around a quarter of a million landworkers lost their jobs and a government report revealed that the wages of those who remained had fallen during a period when other workers enjoyed substantial rises in income.

The village was no longer at the heart of national life. Around the middle of the century the headlong charge into industrialization had caused the urban population of England to exceed that of the countryside. With the village now at the periphery of affairs, its industries gone or withering and its people weak and lacking in influence, it became a place of myth and sentiment, an idyllic alternative to the fumes and grime, greed and savagery of the world where fortunes were made. After all, the wise old ploughman with his homilies and local lore was a much more acceptable symbol of the national character than the silver-tongued stockbroker or the coarse-mouthed mill owner – or most of the other self-seekers who had made the country what it was.

Soon, with the coming of war in 1914, the myth of village England would be inflated, elaborated and enshrined. Men who were prepared to give their lives in service needed to feel there was a just

The end of the nineteenth century saw a depression in the countryside and many farm workers found themselves unemployed. This hiring fair at Burford, Oxfordshire, was photographed about 1900.

cause for dying. The image of the nation which was offered to them was not one of soot-stained terraces or straggling suburbs but of the mythical rural havens, which, in fact, the volunteers proved remarkably eager to forsake. Hardly any of them could have offered a coherent explanation of what the Great War was actually about. Like their village forefathers, they had a crude and unquestioning patriotism which seemed to endure no matter how badly they were actually treated by the motherland. When the volunteers from village England recorded their reasons for enlisting, romance took something of a beating. They went because there was no work in the village. They went because the army offered them warm clothes, dry boots and three square meals a day. They went because this was their best opportunity to see something of the world beyond the confines of the parish. No man who had worked for masters like those East Anglian farmers of Scottish descent could find much to fear in the tyranny of the sergeant major.

When tragedy hit the village, it tended to hit hard, bringing bereavement to a whole string of houses along the high street. When they left home, the men went in waggons or on foot to join their local regiment, with men from the Yorkshire Dales, for example, heading for Richmond and the Green Howards. Friends from the same village rubbed shoulders in the trenches – sound military policy, since a man was unlikely to turn and run so long as there might be survivors to tell of his shame in the pub and workplace back home – so that when the regiment suffered losses from German fire, then a village might lose the cream of its menfolk in a matter of minutes. There were plenty of villages like Buckland in Berkshire, which yielded 79 recruits from a population of just 302, or Barley in Hertfordshire, which gave up 141 service men from its 500 inhabitants and had almost half of them slain, including 9 members of one family and 7 of another.

On returning from the trenches, the wounded found that English farming was enjoying a recovery – as farming always did in times of war. Poor land which had not been cultivated since the Napoleonic wars was back under the plough, but now much of the work was being performed by the women and children of the village. Not only had many of the men gone to Flanders, so too had the heavy horses – and this situation gave the farmer an even greater incentive to explore the possibilities of mechanization. Sadly, the boom lasted no longer than the war. Soon the countryside was back in crisis and the farm labourer's wages, which had climbed to £3 per week in 1918, shrank to just £1 16s. (£1.80). Tractors appeared and the payroll withered. Soon there were machines for ditching, drilling, milking, picking, digging and most other tasks, while the ancient crafts, like hedge-laying, which could not be mechanized, were simply neglected. Village life declined until another war revitalized farming. Meanwhile, village cottages could be bought for much less than a good motor car. The villages were dying. The crisis which had begun by enclosure two centuries earlier now seemed to be reaching its grim conclusion. The rural communities had been reduced, transformed and demoralized. The old bonds of obligation and co-operation had been shattered. The village was on its knees.

11 Today and tomorrow

We have found that the English village is not as timeless and rock-like as we have been led to believe; it is changeable and fragile. By glancing at the evidence of prehistory, and also at those parts of the country where hamlets and farmsteads still rule the rural roost, we discover that villages are not an inevitable part of the countryside. There has to be a good reason for the existence of villages, otherwise people will simply live elsewhere. For centuries the main reason was provided by farming of a special type – a type which involved complicated arrangements for co-operation, for sharing decisions and for submitting to custom and master. Eventually the basis for this existence was swept away by the decay of feudalism and by enclosure. Yet hands were still required to work the land, farmworkers needed homes and the village dormitories already existed – and so the villages outlived the commons and the strip fields which had nourished them. In time, however, machines replaced hands and then the village lost its reason for being. It had always been bound and wedded to the meadows, ploughlands, woods and pastures which embraced it. When the bond was broken, the village was irrelevant. It might just as well die.

During the agricultural decay of the Depression years, many villages did seem to be withering around their aged occupants. But very few of them died. Salvation arose from the same phenomenon which had robbed the wheelwright of his trade, bankrupted the village tailor and sealed the fate of many grocers. The mobility that came with the age of the train, the bus and the motor car not only allowed villagers to shop in town but it also allowed townsfolk to live in the country. People whose forbears had quit village England

New houses in old villages are an emotive issue. The materials will not be local, the style will not be regional, the new inhabitants will not be part of the life of the village.

generations or centuries earlier now returned to enjoy the tranquillity, the greenery and the myth. They arrived like confident colonists in a strange land – a land peopled by natives with curious beliefs and customs, quaint dialects, a peculiar innocence and an ignorance of so many subjects deemed essential for survival. When the locals behaved as rustic locals were expected to behave, they could be regarded as colourful, wise and worthy of patronage. At other times, they were at best a disappointment and at worst a downright nuisance.

The locals, meanwhile, regarded the newcomers with mixed feelings, though all the village tradespeople welcomed their arrival. This optimism proved to be misplaced, for it was soon found that the commuters did their shopping in the supermarkets of the towns where they worked. Village family businesses continued to fold. Journalist Edward Pilkington has cited the case of Snitterfield near Stratford as an example. In 1940 it supported a shoemaker, wheelwright, blacksmith, saddler, hurdle maker and four shops. In 1986 it still maintained a shop, a sub-post office and two petrol stations, but now even the shop and post office have gone.

As the commuter colony grows, it soon emerges that the village contains two nations: different nations, with interests that are directly opposed. Cottages and farmsteads which once housed patrons of rural shops and services are now occupied by two-car families of newcomers who use neither the village stores nor the local bus services. The old villagers who lack their own transport are stranded as public services peter out, partly for want of patronage. Subsidies have been removed from rural bus services and deregulation has had some sorry consequences. In my own Nidderdale village the non-car-owning natives are less mobile than people in this parish have been for centuries. Even in Georgian times all but the poorest of farmer-weavers owned or had use of a horse and Victorian diaries show just how widely and frequently people travelled on horseback. In the 1950s villagers could reach town by train or by a cheap, hourly and reliable bus service. The railway line closed long ago and now the buses are expensive, infrequent and unreliable. In countless places the old villagers are marooned, while the local shops and post offices have gone forever.

The greatest source of conflict between the divided communities of village England concerns housing. There are many old village householders who have been delighted to sell their home to newcomers, amazed at the price that the rickety cottage realized and pleased to migrate to the larger amenities of the town. For those who

Finchingfield, in Essex, seems to embody popular ideas of the 'Olde Worlde' village, but really the fossilized medieval textiles town is so inundated by visitors and colonized by affluent commuters that few vestiges of old village life survive.

choose to remain and set up house in the ancestral village, the inability to compete in the housing market is a perpetual source of outrage and anguish. Throughout most of the country no toe-hold in the village can be bought for less than £60,000 – and on farm worker's wages this figure might just as well be £60 million.

The village can no longer shelter its own.

Once council housing estates were built as sanctuaries for those born in the village, but which councils will now build village housing in the knowledge that these houses can be bought by their occupants and resold to outsiders at great profit? In the 'popular' parts of England, former council houses can sell for upwards of £70,000, and in places with severe shortages of cheap rural housing some now serve as holiday cottages.

The homegrown poor of the village have become the pawns of the property developers. Genuine needs for sheltered housing for the elderly and for cheap housing for first-time buyers become levers used to prise planning permission from the authorities. In one village there was a long-standing need for a couple of retirement flats or cottages. The council attempted to buy the necessary land from a prominent local worthy, but the price was too high. Then another farmer offered to provide some land – so long as five times as many additional new houses could be built there to give him some profit from the deal. The vicar posted a petition in the village shop and parish councillors added their voices to the pro-housing lobby. Although the proposal seemed to breach most strategic planning principles, few villagers were prepared to object. The authorities approved the scheme to add a high-density housing extension to the village boundary. Shortly afterwards the council decided that it could no longer afford to pay for the local retirement component of the scheme, but the remainder of the development goes ahead.

Having secured a niche in the village, the newcomer then seeks to preserve the place or, better still, to mould it until it accords more closely with the village of popular mythology. His house may have been built in 1990, but he is going to do his level best to ensure that none are built in 1995. He, his wife and their neighbours are successful, articulate and well connected. Freemasons, rotarians, chambers of commerce, the professions and government are all represented in the community. Where the old community was artless, inarticulate and easy prey for any passing shark, the new one is organized, informed and influential. There is a village society with words like 'preservation' or 'heritage' in its name. It circulates a newsletter which urges people to clip their hedges, when not broadcasting news of the latest planning application to send shudders down the collective spine of this spruced-up corner of commuterdom. With each new window box, set of shutters, pair of Laura Ashley curtains and carved name board on the green, the myth approaches reality and the reality of village life retreats.

In a sense, the members of the new community are genuine conservationists. Without their organized opposition, village after village would be engulfed by unsightly and discordant property developments – particularly in recent times when authorities may be afraid to resist affluent developers for fear that they may be obliged to pay the costs of the planning appeal. Yet, what the newcomers fail to realize is that the village was as much a community as a collection of buildings. They may be very adept at conserving structures and spaces, yet they seem to care nothing for the humanity of the old village – a fact which makes their efforts seem empty as well as selfish. Even so, it is hard to imagine how old ways of making a living, of treating neighbours, of communicating about countryside issues, of speaking and of thinking could be conserved. Green belts, conservation areas, listings and so on are excellent instruments for preserving the visual aspects of places, but they are virtually useless as means of conserving *people*. The sad fact remains that the worst enemy of the true-born villager has proved not to be the wicked property developer, the bent councillor or the witless planner but his new neighbour.

What does it all matter? The village as a village was doomed to die whether the commuters colonized it or not. On the slope above the village a massive tractor plies back and forth. The man in the cab works alone. He has no comrades, neighbours or peers to emulate or impress. His instructions erupt suddenly and impersonally from the

two-way radio at his side. He does not sing the folk songs of Shropshire or Devon; instead his music comes from the headphones of his Walkman. He is missing nothing. The lapwing, curlew, lark and corncrake left this countryside long ago. Neither can he hear the clinking of the ranks of ploughshares. The hedges went some time ago to make way for the great combine harvesters. When the hedges went, the soil soon followed, blowing, streaming and drifting away to choke up streams and ditches – the same soil that was tilled, mucked, rested and nurtured by forty generations of village peasants and farmers. Like the men who cared for it, it is going.

The village below neither knows nor cares. Once the tangled lanes radiating towards each meadow, pasture, common, coppice and furlong would fill at dawn and again at dusk as the village workers moved between cottage and field. Now only the dog-walkers know those old lanes. The link between people and the land which gave the village its meaning is broken. What is left is just a shell. It is not an empty shell, yet it is empty of all those things like poverty, comradeship, mutual respect and rural lore that were the essential ingredients of a village. What remains may be vital; a community of a kind, and one day, perhaps, even a vibrant one. Who knows?

Now marooned and with few neighbours left who remember the old rural ways, can the old villagers look back across the generations to a Golden Age of English village life? In truth, there never was one. The best that was ever on offer were the pleasures of the dawn chorus and owls screeching in ink-black skies, of toiling with friends and enjoying their respect and humour and of seeing the harvest safely stacked. Nobody ever promised ease, warmth, sufficiency and security. And nobody ever gave it.

Ideas for further reading

The following books are especially recommended because they provide detailed information on particular aspects of the village story.

Beresford, M. W., *Lost Villages of England*, 1954
Beresford, M. W., and J. K. S. St Joseph, *Medieval England: An Aerial Survey*, 1979
Blythe, R., *Akenfield*, 1969
Chapelot, J. and R. Fossier, *The Village and House in the Middle Ages*, 1985
Cobbett, W., *Cottage Economy*, 1979
Cook, O., *English Cottages and Farmhouses*, 1982
Coulton, G. G., *The Medieval Village*, 1926
Darley, G., *Villages of Vision*, 1978
Evans, G. E., *Ask the Fellows who Cut the Hay*, 1965
Gough, R., *The History of Myddle*, 1981
Hallam, E. M., *Domesday Book Through Nine Centuries*, 1986
Hammond, J. L., and B., *The Village Labourer*, 1978
Homans, G. C., *English Villagers of the Thirteenth Century*, 1975
Machin, R., *The Houses of Yetminster*, 1978
Martin, E. W. (ed.), *Country Life in England*, 1966
Muir, R., *The Lost Villages of Britain*, 1982
Muir, R., *Dark Age and Medieval Britain, 400–1350*, 1985
Parker, R., *The Common Stream*, 1975
Randall, G., *The English Parish Church*, 1972
Roberts, B. K., *The Making of the English Village*, 1987
Rodwell, W., *The Archaeology of the English Church*, 1981
Rowley, T., *Villages in the Landscape*, 1978
Samuel, R. (ed.), *Village Life and Labour*, 1975
Steane, J. M., *The Archaeology of Medieval England and Wales*, 1985
Steer, F. W. (ed.) *Farm and Cottage Inventories, 1635–1749*, 1969
Taylor, C., *Village and Farmstead*, 1983

Photographic acknowledgments

All the photographs are the author's except the following: p 15 (top) Howard Brooks; pp 51 and 188 Edwin Smith; pp 202, 203 and 206 Museum of English Rural Life, Reading; p 213 Tobey Museum, Burford; pp 70, 204 and 205 Lee Frost.

Index

J

I

H